The Bahá'í Faith

**Mary Perkins
Philip Hainsworth**

Ward Lock Educational

ISBN 0 7062 3939 3

First published 1980

Approved by the National Spiritual Assembly of the Bahá'is of the United Kingdom

Set in 11 on 12 point Times Roman
by David Green Printers Ltd. Kettering, Northamptonshire
for Ward Lock Educational
116 Baker Street,
London W1M 2BB
A member of the Pentos Group

Contents

3   How the Bahá'ís live   62

Introduction

The Bahá'í Faith is the religion of the followers of Bahá'u'lláh. The name Bahá'u'lláh is Arabic for 'The glory of God', and a Bahá'í is a follower of Bahá'u'lláh.

The Bahá'í Faith is the youngest of the world's living religions. It began in Írán in 1844 and is now, in 1979, established in over 102,000 centres scattered through 343 countries, dependent territories and major island groups. Bahá'í literature has been translated into more than 670 different languages.

Although it began in a Muslim country, Írán, the Bahá'í Faith is as distinct from Islám as Christianity is from Judaism, and it is a world religion which has spread to almost every corner of the globe within its first 130 years. It includes within its membership a cross-section of the human race and offers to the whole of mankind a way to peace, love and unity which is satisfying, challenging and inspiring.

The Bahá'í International Community is an international non-governmental organization cooperating closely with the United Nations to achieve the goals of world peace, universal human rights and the full economic and social development of the peoples of this planet. It was granted consultative status with the Economic and Social Council (ECOSOC) in 1970 and has permanent representatives at the United Nations headquarters in New York and in Geneva and with the United Nations Environment Programme (UNEP) in Nairobi.

The human race, so rich in its diversity of colour, culture, tradition and experience must, if it is to be united in carrying forward an ever-advancing world civilization, be offered a new way of life, simple in its basic features but sufficiently complex in its detailed application to cater for all its needs and aspirations.

The Bahá'í Faith offers this new way of life. This book serves as an introduction to the Faith; it does not in any way attempt to deal with all the many aspects of this new world Faith but it is a fairly comprehensive textbook written to give enough of its history, teachings and objectives to encourage further study.

It will be a study, we believe, which will be highly rewarding and not a little exciting.

Mary Perkins and Philip Hainsworth

Acknowledgments

The authors and publishers would like to thank the following for their help in supplying the photographs which illustrate this book: the Bahá'í World Centre; Ted Cardell; Adam Thorne; Hari Docherty and many other kind friends; and Messrs George Ronald, Publisher, for permission to use the Map of Persia and to Rushton Sabit and Lois Hainsworth for their invaluable help and suggestions when checking the manuscript for accuracy.

We also express gratitude to the National Spiritual Assembly of the Bahá'ís of the United Kingdom whose Reviewing Panel gave the manuscript their approval.

How the Bahá'í Faith began

The land of Írán
Írán consists of a large plateau surrounded on all sides by high
mountains with a great salt desert at its centre. To the west is the
plain of the Tigris, to the east the Indus valley, to the north the
Caspian Sea and the Turanian Desert, and to the south the Persian
Gulf and the Indian Ocean.

In order to appreciate the environment into which the Bahá'í
Faith was born, it is important to realize that in the early 1800s the
whole area of the Middle East was in a state of political, economic
and social decline.

The people of Írán, who in previous centuries had produced great
civilizations, were by 1800 weakened and isolated from the main
currents of world affairs. A few people lived in great luxury while
many suffered through poverty, disease and ignorance. Attempts at
reform were hindered by widespread corruption, bribery and
malpractice on the part of the government.

Most of the people of Írán were Muslim but there were also
people of the Zoroastrian, Jewish and Christian Faiths living in the
country. There was much mutual hatred and intolerence between the
followers of these different faiths. Yet Írán, or 'Persia' as it was
known, was of great significance to both Muslims and Christians,
having been mentioned in a number of places in their Scriptures.
The Reverend H. Bonar, a Christian scholar writing on Biblical
prophecy in the early part of the nineteenth century, accepted the
prophecies about Assyria, Elam and Persia, but confessed to being
unable to explain why these places should, 'in the latter days', be so
blessed.

The search for the Promised One
In the late eighteenth century, a learned and saintly Muslim called
Shaykh Aḥmad set out on a journey from his home on an island in
the Persian Gulf. He was prompted to travel by his conviction that
'the Promised One' mentioned in the Islamic scriptures would
shortly appear on earth.

Shaykh Aḥmad believed that this holy messenger of God whose

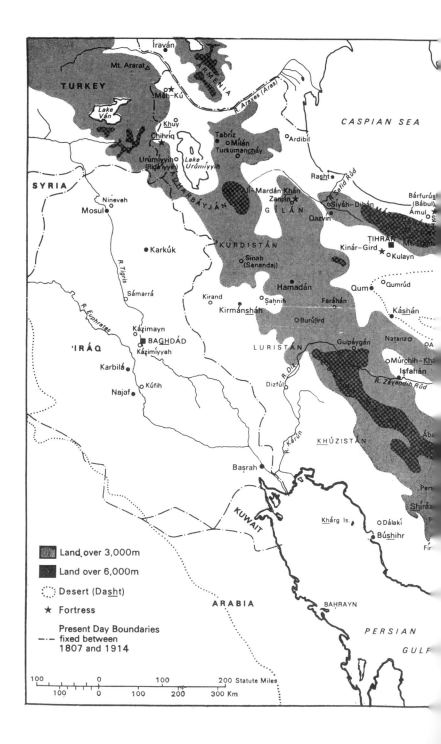

Land over 3,000m

Land over 6,000m

Desert (Da<u>sh</u>t)

★ Fortress

Present Day Boundaries
—·— fixed between
1807 and 1914

8

PERSIA IN THE NINETEENTH CENTURY

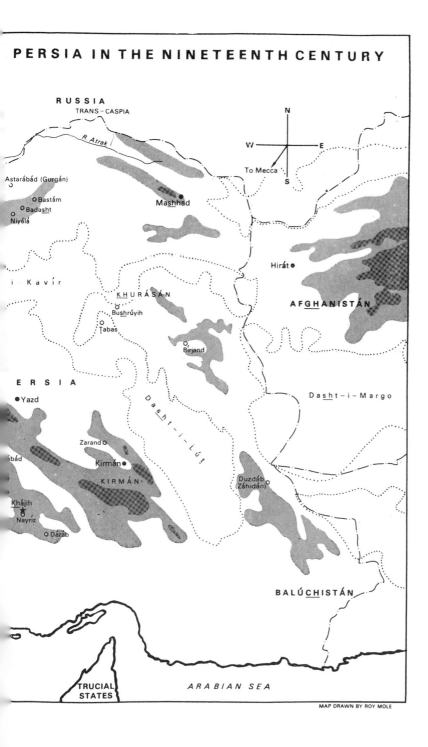

RUSSIA
TRANS-CASPIA

R Atrak

N
W — E
S

To Mecca

Astarábád (Gurgán)

○ Bastám
○ Badasht
Niyálá

Mashhad

Hirát ●

i   K a v í r

KHURÁSÁN

ö Bushrúyih
○ Tabas

AFGHANISTÁN

○ Birjand

E R S I A
● Yazd

Dasht-i-Margo

Zarand ○

íbád

Kirmán ●

Da s h t – i – L ú t

KIRMÁN

Duzdáb
(Záhidán) ○

Khájih
★
Nayríz

○ Dáráb

BALÚCHISTÁN

TRUCIAL
STATES

ARABIAN SEA

MAP DRAWN BY ROY MOLE

9

coming was prophesied was a great world teacher expected by all the peoples of the world. His appearance on earth, Shaykh Aḥmad believed, would mark the beginning of a new age for humanity, an age when the different religions would become united and all men live in peace.

Shaykh Aḥmad travelled first to Najaf and then to Karbilá, a city holy to the Muslims. The Imám Ḥusayn, the grandson of the Prophet Muḥammad, had been martyred at Karbilá. In Karbilá Shaykh Aḥmad began to preach and teach but later moved into Írán. A young man named Siyyid Káẓim (Siyyid is a title meaning that the person is a descendant of the Prophet Muḥammad) heard of Shaykh Aḥmad's teachings and travelled across the country to meet him.

Shaykh Aḥmad greeted the young man joyfully. He knew that he had found someone with whom he could share all his knowledge and the longings of his heart. Together they studied and prayed, travelled and taught.

Shaykh Aḥmad appointed Siyyid Káẓim as his successor and after his teacher's death, Siyyid Káẓim remained at Karbilá and continued to teach there. One of those who came to learn from the Siyyid was a young man called Mullá Ḥusayn. Mullá Ḥusayn was a pure-hearted and eager seeker after truth and a brilliant scholar. Siyyid Káẓim knew that he could trust Mullá Ḥusayn completely; he had great confidence in the young student's abilities and sent him on a special mission to Írán.

In due course Siyyid Káẓim became increasingly aware of the imminence of the dawn of a new Revelation and endeavoured to lift the veil that might prevent his disciples from recognizing God's Treasure when He was revealed. He told them:

He is of noble lineage... a descendant of the Prophet of God... He is young in age and possessed of innate knowledge. His learning is derived not from the teachings of Shaykh Aḥmad, but from God. My knowledge is but a drop compared with the immensity of his knowledge, my attainments a speck of dust in the face of the wonders of his grace and power... He is of medium height, abstains from smoking and is of extreme devoutness and piety.[1]

Siyyid Káẓim urged his followers to scatter far and wide to look for the Promised One, to give up their careers, their belongings, even, if necessary, their lives, in their search.

Mullá Ḥusayn returned from Írán to find that his teacher had died. He spent forty days in prayer and fasting, preparing his heart for the journey of search. Some of his fellow students, inspired by his example, began to do the same. When the forty days were over, Mullá Ḥusayn set out on his journey with two young companions, his brother and his nephew, who were both barely twenty years old.

The three young men left Karbilá with no clear idea of where they should first look. They prayed earnestly for guidance from God, and Mullá Ḥusayn found himself being drawn, as if by a magnet, towards S͟híráz, a city in the south of Írán. S͟híráz is a beautiful city, famous for its poets, its flower gardens and nightingales.

Mullá Ḥusayn and his companions arrived at the city gate late one afternoon. They were dusty, hungry and tired. Mullá Ḥusayn sent his companions on ahead into the city and lingered for a while outside the city gate, wondering what he would find in S͟híráz that might lead him to the Promised One.

As he stood outside the city gate, a young man with a radiant face and wearing a green turban (an indication that he was descended from the Prophet Muḥammad) approached him. The young stranger smiled and welcomed Mullá Ḥusayn to S͟híráz as if he were a long-lost friend. His radiance and serenity, his purity, courtesy and dignity made a strong impression on the travel-weary Mullá Ḥusayn who was filled with joy in the stranger's company. The young stranger invited Mullá Ḥusayn to enter the city and refresh himself at his house. Mullá Ḥusayn explained that he had sent his companions on ahead and that they would be waiting for him.

'Commit them to the care of God. He will surely protect and watch over them' said the young stranger and he escorted Mullá Ḥusayn into the city of S͟híráz.

The Declaration of the Báb
The young man who met Mullá Ḥusayn outside S͟híráz was named Siyyid 'Alí-Muhammad. He was descended through both of his parents from the Prophet Muḥammad. He was born on October 20, 1819; his father had died when he was young and he had been brought up by an uncle. When this uncle first sent his nephew to school, the teacher sent him home again, saying that there was nothing that he could teach the boy that he did not already know. 'Alí-Muḥammad had an extraordinary innate knowledge that he had not learnt from books or from any other person. This innate knowledge enabled him to answer the most difficult questions which his teachers could not themselves answer.

12

In his early teens 'Alí-Muḥammad began to work for his uncle as a merchant at the port of Búshihr and in Shíráz. He was soon respected for his modesty and fairmindedness in business, for his devotion and humility, for the depth and breadth of his knowledge and for the sweetness and nobility of his character. At the time that he met Mullá Ḥusayn he had been working for fewer than ten years; he had married his mother's cousin and his baby son had died when he was one year old. This was the young merchant who met Mullá Ḥusayn and then led him courteously to his home, a modest house in a quite corner of Shíráz. Mullá Ḥusayn felt a growing sense of peace and happiness in the company of his host.

It was time for the evening prayers observed by all Muslims. The two young men knelt in prayer and Mullá Ḥusayn prayed earnestly that this strange encounter might somehow help him in his search for the Promised One. When they had said their prayers, they sat and spoke together. Overwhelmed by the great kindness, dignity and courtesy of his host, Mullá Ḥusayn unburdened the deepest longings of his heart. He spoke of the journey and search that he had undertaken. 'Alí-Muḥammad listened attentively and then asked whether Siyyid Káẓim had given any indications as to how his followers would recognize the Promised One. Mullá Ḥusayn repeated the description given by Siyyid Káẓim: 'He is of a pure lineage, is of illustrious descent. . . He is endowed with innate knowledge . . . is free from bodily deficiency . . .'[2]

There was silence in the room for a few moments when Mullá Ḥusayn finished speaking. Then Siyyid 'Alí-Muḥammad spoke quietly but in tones of strength and power. 'Behold all these signs are manifest in Me.'[3]

Mullá Ḥusayn was greatly surprised. He began to protest, saying that the Promised One he sought was a man of unsurpassed holiness and the Cause he was to reveal was a Cause of tremendous power, but even as he spoke he experienced a sense of awe and remorse. He ceased to protest. He eagerly took out a paper which he had written some years earlier. It was an attempt he had made to explain some of the most difficult teachings of Shaykh Aḥmad and Siyyid Káẓim. He asked his host to look at the paper. The Siyyid read it rapidly and explained, simply and clearly, all the difficulties that Mullá Ḥusayn had encountered in writing the paper. He then said, as Mullá Ḥusayn listened with astonishment and joy, 'Now is the time to reveal the commentary on the Súrih of Joseph'.[4]

A fine example of calligraphy of this period

The Súrih of Joseph (súrih means chapter) is a chapter in the Qur'án. Mullá Ḥusayn had once asked Siyyid Káẓim to write a commentary on that chapter. 'This is, verily, beyond me' Siyyid Káẓim had replied. 'He, that great One, who comes after me will, unasked, reveal it for you.'[5]

As Mullá Ḥusayn recalled these words spoken by his teacher, his host took up his pen and began to write. He chanted the words in a melodious voice as he wrote them down. He did not pause in his chanting or his writing until a whole chapter, the Súrih of Mulk, was completed. Mullá Ḥusayn sat listening, enraptured by the sweetness of his voice and the power of the words he uttered.

The declaration that he was indeed the Promised One was made by the young merchant of Shíráz to Mullá Ḥusayn two hours and eleven minutes after sunset on 22 May 1844. It is a date and time that is celebrated by Bahá'ís as the beginning of a new era in human history.

'O Thou who art the first to believe in Me!' were the exact words he spoke to Mullá Ḥusayn. 'Verily I say, I am the Báb, the Gate of God.'[6]

The name Báb means 'the gate' and the Báb claimed to be the Gate to a new age of peace and universal brotherhood. He said that his mission was to foretell the coming of another, much greater Messenger who would shortly appear. He referred to this great Messenger as 'He whom God shall make manifest' and spoke of him as one who would unite all men and establish a just and lasting peace on earth.

All through that night Mullá Ḥusayn sat and listened, oblivious of time and of the companions who awaited him, as the Báb continued. While the city slept around them, the Báb warned Mullá Ḥusayn that he must tell no one, not even his companions, of what he had seen or heard.

'Eighteen souls must' said the Báb 'in the beginning, spontaneously and of their own accord, accept me and recognize the truth of my revelation. Unwarned and uninvited, each of these must seek independently to find me.'[7]

As the call to morning prayer was raised from the minarets of Shíráz, Mullá Ḥusayn left the house of the Báb. Joy, wonder, excitement and awe filled his soul.

'The knowledge of his revelation' he said, 'had galvanized my being. I felt possessed of such courage and power that were the world, all its peoples and potentates, to rise against me, I would alone and undaunted, withstand their onslaught. The universe seemed but a handful of dust in my grasp.'[8]

Forty more days passed before the other disciples of the Báb began to recognize him. Gradually, spontaneously and completely independently of one another, some in fasting and prayer, some in dreams and visions, they recognized the station of the young merchant of Shíráz. They had all been students of Siyyid Kázim and seemed to be attracted to Shíráz by that same power that had drawn Mullá Husayn to the city. The last to arrive was Quddús. He reached Shíráz dust-stained and travel weary. On seeing Mullá Husayn in the street, he eagerly asked for news of the search. Mullá Husayn tried to pacify him, but without success, for Quddús had seen the Báb walking in the street.

'Why seek you to hide him from me?' Quddús cried out to the astonished Mullá Husayn. 'I can recognize him by his gait. I confidently testify that none besides him, whether in the East or in the West, can claim to be the Truth. None other can manifest the power and majesty that radiate from his holy person.'[9]

The Báb called together those disciples who had reached Shíráz and told them to scatter through Írán to spread his teachings and to prepare men's hearts for the coming of 'Him whom God shall make manifest'. He stressed the great responsibility that they carried, urged caution and moderation and warned that they would face torture and death as a reward for their efforts.

'I am preparing you' he told them 'for the advent of a mighty Day. Exert your utmost endeavour that, in the world to come, I who am now instructing you, may, before the mercy-seat of God, rejoice in your deeds and glory in your achievements... Scatter throughout the length and breadth of this land, and, with steadfast feet and sanctified hearts, prepare the way for his coming. Heed not your weaknesses and frailty; fix your gaze upon the invincible power of the Lord, your God, the Almighty. Has he not, in past days, caused Abraham, in spite of his seeming helplessness, to triumph over the forces of Nimrod? Has he not enabled Moses, whose staff was his only companion, to vanquish Pharaoh and his hosts? Has he not established the ascendancy of Jesus, poor and lowly as he was in the eyes of men, over the combined forces of the Jewish people? Has he not subjected the barbarous and militant tribes of Arabia to the holy and transforming discipline of Muhammad, his prophet? Arise in his name, put your trust wholly in him, and be assured of ultimate victory.'[10]

The Ministry of the Báb

The followers of the Báb set out joyfully to spread his teachings. The message that they gave sparked off a tremendous excitement in Irán. People thronged to hear them and the fame of the Báb grew swiftly. Rich and poor, simple and learned, town-dweller and villager alike wanted to know more. A number of learned and highly respected religious teachers became followers of the Báb. The authorities became alarmed and reacted swiftly. When Quddús and an elderly companion began to spread the Báb's teachings in Shíráz, they were seized by the authorities of that city, their beards were burned, their noses pierced, through this incision a cord was passed and with this halter they were led through the streets. They were beaten and sent out of Shíráz with a warning that if they tried to return they would by crucified.

The Báb was put under house arrest as a wave of passionate enquiry rocked the country. The Sháh sent Vaḥíd, a most trusted adviser, and a learned, influential and highly respected man, to investigate the cause of the excitement. Vaḥíd became a devoted follower of the Báb after three interviews with him and at once began to spread his teachings.

The Grand Vizier, the chief minister of the Sháh, became extremely worried. He was frightened that the Báb might influence the Sháh if they should meet. He therefore imprisoned the Báb at Máh-Kú in the north of the country.

The people living around Máh-Kú were simple farmers, ignorant of the world beyond their own hills and hostile to outsiders.

The prison governor was at first hostile to the Báb but soon realized that he was no ordinary person. He began to love and revere the Báb. The local farmers felt the influence of the prisoner in their lives. They came to stand beneath the prison walls in hope of hearing him chant his prayers. They asked for his blessing on their daily work and called on each other to speak the truth in his name. Visitors came from far and wide, the governor allowed them in and became daily more devoted to the prisoner in his charge.

Again the Grand Vizier became alarmed and sent the Báb to a more remote prison at Chihríq. The governor of Chihríq prison was the Sháh's own brother-in-law. He was harsh and unpredictable and at the outset acted with great severity but he too yielded to the fascination of the Báb. Again the local people began to love and revere him. Again the visitors streamed to Chihríq. One visitor was a man from India who reached Chihríq dressed as a hermit. He had

View of the Prison of Máh-Kú. The Castle is at the base of the overhanging rock above the village

been a prince in his own country but had seen the Báb in a vision and had given up wealth and position to look for him. The Báb sent him back to India to spread the teachings.

Persecution of the Báb's followers increased as the teachings spread in Írán. The Báb's first disciples and hundreds of those who had responded to their message were cruelly tortured and killed. Had they recanted their faith, they would have lived. The Báb's own uncle, who had reared and educated him, was killed because of his belief in the mission of his nephew. The Báb was filled with anguish and sorrow at the deaths of his followers. While in prison at Chihríq he wrote down a great many of his teachings. He knew that his own death would come soon.

In 1850, unable to stop the spread of the movement, the authorities decided to execute the Báb in an attempt to stamp out the heresy once and for all. Thus, after three years of relative freedom and three of captivity, the Báb's six-year ministry was hastening to its spectacular climax.

The Execution of the Báb

The Báb was taken to Tabríz. As he was led into the city a young man threw himself at the Báb's feet and begged to be allowed to die with him. The young man was arrested and condemned to die with the Báb.

On his last night on earth the Báb was radiant and joyful. He knew that his mission was accomplished despite all opposition. Early next morning the Báb was interrupted as he was dictating last minute instructions to a companion. Soldiers sent from those responsible for the Báb's imprisonment, attempted to hurry the Báb away but he spoke to the official in charge saying: 'Not until I have said to him all those things I wish to say can any earthly power silence me. Though all the world be armed against me, yet shall they be powerless to deter me from fulfilling, to the last word, my intention.'[11]

In a sequence of events remarkably similar to those experienced over eighteen centuries earlier when Jesus received his sentence without fair trial, the Báb was taken to the homes of three eminent religious leaders to obtain the necessary death warrants. Not one of them condescended to face the Báb, as the documents were already written, signed and sealed.

The Báb was led through the crowded streets where about 10,000 people had thronged to Tabríz to watch him die.

The Prison at Chihríq

18

The leader of the regiment ordered to execute the Báb was a Christian named Sám Khán. He was impressed by the goodness and humility of the Báb and was deeply troubled by the task ahead of him.

'I entertain no ill-will against you,' he told the Báb. 'If your Cause be the Cause of Truth, enable me to free myself from the obligation to shed your blood.'

'Follow your instructions,' the Báb replied 'and if your intention be sincere, the Almighty is surely able to relieve you from your perplexity.'[12]

The Báb and his young companion were suspended by ropes against the wall of the barrack square and 750 soldiers of Sám Khán's regiment took aim at them and fired. When the smoke from the fire cleared a great shout went up from the crowd. The Báb was nowhere to be seen and the young man who had been tied up with him was standing unharmed. There was a frantic search for the Báb. They found him finishing his instructions which had earlier been interrupted.

'I have finished my conversation', the Báb told those who found him, 'Now you may proceed to fulfil your intention.'[13]

Sám Khán ordered his own regiment out of the barracks and refused to have anything more to do with the execution of the Báb. Another regiment was called in. This time the bodies of the Báb and his companion were shattered to pieces, though their faces were hardly marred.

The execution took place at noon on 9 July 1850.

At the same hour a fierce storm broke over the city. Strong winds blew and dust darkened the skies for the rest of the day. The bodies of the Báb and his companion were thrown outside the city walls and forty soldiers were set on guard so that the followers of the Báb should not rescue them. Despite this guard, the Báb's followers managed to rescue the remains of the bodies and hide them in a place of safety.

The Báb and His Message
The Báb claimed to be the bearer of an independent revelation from God and the herald of a greater messenger than himself. He changed the Islamic laws and ceremonies concerned with prayer, fasting, marriage, divorce and inheritance. In his writings his constant theme is the coming of 'Him whom God shall make manifest'. He extols the greatness of the messenger who is to come and urges his

followers to hurry to him when he appears even if they have to crawl to him over snow.

'I myself am,' the Báb wrote, 'but the first servant to believe in him and in his signs, and to partake of the sweet savours of his words from the first fruits of the paradise of his knowledge.'[14]

The Báb believed that God's next messenger would appear very shortly after his own death.

Two years after the Báb was shot, two of his young followers, crazy with grief and despair at the death of their leader, attempted to assassinate the Sháh. The weapon they chose was quite unsuitable for their purpose and the Sháh was only slightly wounded. Their act triggered off a wave of persecution against the Bábís. The authorities whipped up popular support for a campaign of vengeance and determined to rid themselves of the Bábís.

Men, women and children were tortured and killed in ghastly massacres. Foreign residents in Írán kept to their houses for fear of witnessing savage scenes of torture and killing in the streets and the most able and distinguished of the Báb's followers, a man named Bahá'u'lláh, was thrown into prison.

Bahá'u'lláh

Bahá'u'lláh means in Arabic 'The Glory of God' and was a name mentioned by the Báb. Bahá'u'lláh was born Mírzá Husayn 'Alí into one of the leading noble families of Írán. His father was a leading minister at the court of the Sháh. He was born in Ṭihrán on November 12, 1817.

Bahá'u'lláh was surrounded from birth by riches, comfort and elegance. His clothes were of the finest silk, his food the best that wealth and position could provide. His family owned fine houses. In common with his young noble contemporaries, Bahá'u'lláh received instruction in the main teachings of Islám, the literature and poetry of Írán and was taught calligraphy. Bahá'u'lláh, like the Báb, possessed an extraordinary knowledge that was not gained from a teacher or from any books. Men marvelled at the breadth and depth of his knowledge and at his exceptional powers of logic and reasoning. At the age of seven he represented his father in a property dispute at the court of the Sháh and won the case for which he argued.

His exceptional knowledge did not make him proud. He was modest and genial, sympathetic and very kind. His tastes were simple. He loved the countryside, birds, trees, flowers and animals

20

and preferred to spend his time in the country rather than at court. He did not spend his money on personal luxuries but on helping the poor and needy. He married young, as was the custom at the time. His wife was from a very wealthy family but her tastes were similar to her husband's. Together they worked to help those less fortunate than themselves. Their doors were always open to those in need of food, shelter and help. They were given the names 'The Father and Mother of the poor'. When Bahá'u'lláh's father died, his position at court was offered to his son but Bahá'u'lláh refused to accept it.

In the summer of 1844, just three months after the Báb declared his mission, Mullá Husayn carried to Ṭihrán a scroll of the Báb's writing and saw that it reached the hands of Bahá'u'lláh. On reading the scroll, Bahá'u'lláh immediately recognized the claims of the Báb and became his follower at the age of twenty-seven. Bahá'u'lláh never met the Báb but was in constant correspondence with him and he gave whole-hearted support to the spread of the Báb's teachings. In so doing, he put himself on the side of a little-known movement which was directly opposed to the privileges of his own class.

While the Báb was in prison, Bahá'u'lláh lent every possible assistance to his persecuted followers. He was twice imprisoned and once deliberately drew the anger of a mob upon himself rather than allow his companions to suffer. He was beaten and pelted with stones. Undaunted and with tireless energy, Bahá'u'lláh supported, advised and assisted the persecuted Bábís. When the Báb knew that he would soon die, he sent to Bahá'u'lláh his pens, seals and papers. It was at Bahá'u'lláh's initiative and on his explicit instructions that the remains of the Báb were removed from Tabríz to Tihrán and hidden in a place of safety. In the days following the attempt on the Sháh's life, Bahá'u'lláh was a guest of the Grand Vizier. His friends begged him to hide until the tumult was over, but Bahá'u'lláh refused to do this. Instead, he rode towards the army camp where his own seizure and arrest were being planned.

Bahá'u'lláh was stripped of his outer garments and was put in chains. He was made to walk, bare-headed and bare-footed under the midday sun, to prison in Ṭihrán. A large crowd had gathered to hurl stones and insults at him. Bahá'u'lláh asked his guards to slow down in order to enable an old woman who wanted to throw a stone, to catch up with the procession.

'Suffer not this woman,' he said, 'to be disappointed. Deny her not what she regards as a meritorious act in the sight of God.' [15]

The prison to which Bahá'u'lláh was taken had originally been a reservoir for one of the public baths of the city. He was led down a pitch-black corridor and down three flights of steps. The prison chamber was dark, damp and verminous. A hundred and fifty fever-ridden men were kept there with scarcely any clothes and no bedding. They were for the most part murderers, highwaymen and robbers. Bahá' u' lláh and a number of other Bábís were chained among them.

Bahá' u' lláh was placed in stocks, and heavy chains were secured over his shoulders so that he could neither stand up nor lie down. The heavy chains cut into his flesh and he bore the marks of them for the rest of his life. For three days they were given no food or drink and when food did reach Bahá' u' lláh, his enemies had poisoned it. The authorities did not dare to execute Bahá' u' lláh as he was held in such high esteem. Each day the guards came to fetch out one of the Bábís to face torture and death. Each time a Bábí went to death from that prison, he came first to ask for Bahá' u' lláh' s blessing before hurrying joyfully to die. Bahá' u' lláh comforted and encouraged all the prisoners. He taught the Bábís to chant prayers as they sat in their chains. First one row would sing 'God is sufficient unto me; He verily is the All-Sufficing! and the other row would reply: ' In him let the trusting trust.'[16] The prisoners sang with such joy and so loudly that the sound of their chanting could be heard by the <u>Sh</u>áh in his nearby palace.

Bahá' u' lláh was kept in the prison under the same conditions for four months. He became very ill, his neck was galled, his back was bent and he could scarcely walk. While in that prison, Bahá' u' lláh had a mystical experience which taught him that he himself was 'the One whom God shall make manifest' the Holy One whose coming the Báb had foretold.

During the days I lay in the prison of Ṭihrán, though the galling weight of the chains and the stench-filled air allowed me but little sleep, still in those infrequent moments of slumber I felt as if something flowed from the crown of my head over my breast, even as a mighty torrent that precipitateth itself upon the earth from the summit of a lofty mountain. Every limb of my body would, as a result, be set afire. At such moments my tongue recited what no man could bear to hear.[17]

---

* Italics are used for quotations from Bahá'i Scripture.

O King! I was but a man like others, asleep upon my couch, when lo, the breezes of the All-Glorious were wafted over me, and taught me the knowledge of all that hath been. This thing is not from me, but from One who is Almighty and All-Knowing. And he bade me lift up my voice between earth and heaven, and for this there befell me what hath caused the tears of every man of understanding to flow... His all-compelling summons hath reached me, and caused me to speak his praise amidst all people.

Later in life, Bahá'u'lláh wrote of this experience in a letter to the Sháh.

Those who had ordered his imprisonment could find not one shred of evidence to prove that Bahá'u'lláh had been an accomplice in the attack on the Sháh. The Russian Minister to the Sháh's court exerted his influence to get Bahá'u'lláh released from prison, offering him asylum in Russia. Reluctantly, the Sháh gave his consent for Bahá'u'lláh's release. Thus in December 1852, the four months' confinement in the abominable pit known as the Síyáh-Chál, came to an end. It was in this subterranean dungeon, however, that Bahá'u'lláh, 'wrapped in its stygian gloom, breathing its fetid air, numbed by its humid and icy atmosphere, his feet in stocks...'[19] had witnessed the real birth of the Bahá'í Revelation.

Bahá'u'lláh was stripped of his wealth and possessions and preferring the edict of banishment imposed by his government to asylum in Russia, was given one month in which to remove himself and his family from the country.

As his property had been confiscated, Bahá'u'lláh was not able to make adequate provision for the journey. It was midwinter and very cold, and his wife Navváb was seven months pregnant. Bahá'u'lláh was ill and the journey to Baghdád took three months. The exiles travelled over snow-covered mountains along rough mule tracks, the nights were spent in primitive shelters without adequate food or bedding and Bahá'u'lláh's wife sold the silver buttons from her few dresses in order to buy flour to feed the children.

Exile in 'Iráq
Bahá'u'lláh arrived in Baghdád, 'Iráq, on 8 April 1853, frail and ill. It had not been thought likely that he would survive the rigours of the journey or live long after it. He did, however, recover his strength and spent ten years in 'Iráq.

His influence was soon felt in the dispirited, confused and

leaderless followers of the Báb he found there. At this, his own brother grew jealous of him, so without a word of warning to anyone, Bahá'u'lláh left the city one night, determined to stay away in order to avoid being a source of conflict and dissension among the Bábís. It was only one year after his arrival in Baghdád.

Bahá'u'lláh spent the next two years living alone as a hermit in the mountains of Kurdistán. The people of Kurdistán were a proud and warlike people, renowned for their hostility to the Persians. Though living in isolation, Bahá'u'lláh soon gained a reputation for his great kindness and wisdom. Learned men of the region sought him out. He was loved and respected by learned and illiterate alike and gradually the fame of the wise and holy man living in the mountains reached Baghdád. Once his family heard of the wise hermit in Kurdistán, they knew that it was Bahá'u'lláh and sent a messenger to beg him to return, which he did exactly two years after his departure (19 March 1856).

In Bahá'u'lláh's absence, the condition of the Bábí community had gone from bad to worse. He spent the next seven years educating and training the Bábís in the basic teachings of the Báb. By precept and example, by his written and spoken words, he effected a transformation in the Bábí community and proved himself the only person capable of ensuring the stability and integrity of the movement. The Bábís became known in the city for the integrity of their character, the purity of their motives and the excellence of their conduct. Bahá'u'lláh and his companions lived simply and austerely. They had very few material possessions but they lived in great joy.

The Kurdish mystics and the other religious teachers who had visited Bahá'u'lláh in the mountains now came to Baghdád to find him. Some of the local religious leaders also became curious and sought him out. Many became his followers. Poets, mystics, government officials and princes sought his company. Those who were sick and suffering came to him, those who sought justice thronged to his door. The great number of visitors and pilgrims included Christians and Jews as well as Muslims.

During the years in Baghdád verses streamed from the pen of Bahá'u'lláh. *The Book of Certitude*, his major theological work, was written in the space of two days and two nights. In Baghdád he wrote *The Hidden Words*, a short but compelling book of spiritual guidance, and *The Seven Valleys,* a mystical work written in response to questions from the Sufi mystics.

With a mandate from the Sháh a concourse of Muslim leaders in

The prison in 'Akká where Bahá'u'lláh was held. The two windows on the right are in the room he occupied

Baghdád, jealous of his growing influence, tried to discredit him and asked him to perform a miracle that would satisfy all concerned. Bahá'u'lláh agreed to perform any miracle they asked but they could not agree on which to request and his challenge was never taken up.

The Iranian consul in Baghdád, alarmed at Bahá'u'lláh's growing fame, began to agitate for his further banishment. He obtained an order of banishment. The Governor of Baghdád admired Bahá'u'lláh greatly and it was only after five successive orders of banishment had reached him that he reluctantly informed Bahá'u'lláh that the Sultan of the Ottoman Empire had ordered Bahá'u'lláh's transfer to Constantinople.

The announcement of Bahá'u'lláh's banishment caused uproar in the city. Hundreds of people crowded into the streets around his house weeping and lamenting his departure. The crush became so great that Bahá'u'lláh moved out of the city to a garden on the far side of the river. He stayed there for twelve days cheering and encouraging his followers. Many of them knew intuitively that he was the one of whom the Báb had spoken but Bahá'u'lláh had never spoken to anyone of his mission. Here, in the garden of Riḍván, he made a formal declaration to some of his followers that he was indeed 'Him whom God shall make manifest', transforming their great sorrow into joy.

This public announcement that he was the 'Promised One' of all religions, that his Faith was for all mankind and that a new Day had dawned in human history, lasted for a period of twelve days, from 21 April to 2 May 1863. It became known as the Festival of Riḍván, commemorated annually throughout the Bahá'í world as the holiest and most significant of all Bahá'í festivals. No fewer than three of the nine Bahá'í Holy Days occur during this Ridván Festival.

Exile in Turkey

Bahá'u'lláh's journey of exile to Constantinople (Istanbul) was a triumphal procession. He was respectfully met and courteously entertained by the officials and notables of the towns and villages through which he passed. In Constantinople his government's ambassador to the city was urged by his rulers in Ṭihrán to stir up hostility against the exiles and the ambassador painted a picture of Bahá'u'lláh as a proud and arrogant person who had no respect for law and who was working to destroy the Ottoman regime.

When Bahá'u'lláh had been only four months in Constantinople, the Iranian and Ottoman rulers cooperated to secure yet another exile. An order was issued demanding his immediate removal to Adrianople (Edirne). It was December and the coldest winter in living memory. Bahá'u'lláh, his family and his companions had to make a hurried departure without adequate provisions. They travelled in rain and storm across a bleak and windswept landscape. The journey took twelve days; they had to make several night marches and arrived in a state of exhaustion.

Bahá'u'lláh spent five years in Adrianople. He was, by this time, officially a prisoner of the Ottoman Empire but no charge was brought against him.

In Adrianople the Faith underwent a severe internal crisis, caused by the jealousy of Bahá'u'lláh's brother, Mírzá Yahyá and another man named Siyyid Muhammad. It was Mírzá Yahyá who had been jealous of Bahá'u'lláh in Baghdád and who had created difficulties in Constantinople. He had now become so consumed with jealousy that he tried to kill Bahá'u'lláh by poisoning his food. Bahá'u'lláh was made very ill by the poison and suffered from the effects of it for the rest of his life.

While in Adrianople, Bahá'u'lláh formally proclaimed his mission to the kings and rulers of the world and its religious leaders. Here, and later in 'Akká he wrote individual letters to the monarchs of Europe in which he called on them to recognize his faith. He also

26

urged them to settle the differences that divided them, to reduce their armaments and take better care of their people.

In a letter from 'Akká to Queen Victoria, Bahá'u'lláh wrote:

'That which the Lord hath ordained as the sovereign remedy and mightiest instrument for the healing of all the world is the union of all its peoples in one universal Cause, one common Faith. This can in no wise by achieved except through the power of a skilled, an all-powerful and inspired Physician.'[20]

It is related that Queen Victoria's comment on reading the letter was 'If this is of God, it will endure; if not, no harm can come of it'.

The mission of Bahá'u'lláh, revealed to him in the Síyáh Chál, Ṭihrán, but kept concealed for ten years, had been publicly announced in the Riḍván Garden, Baghdád, and was now, in the middle of 1868, being proclaimed individually and collectively to the then rulers of the world. Napoleon III; the Czar of Russia; William I of Prussia; Francis-Joseph of Austria; Pope Pius IX; the Sultan of Turkey and the Sháh of Írán were all addressed by Bahá'u'lláh during his Proclamation.

It was during this period in Adrianople that the Bahá'í greeting, 'Alláh-u-Abhá' (God is All-Glorious) came into use, and the followers of Bahá'u'lláh became known as Bahá'ís. The Bahá'ís in Írán and 'Iráq were bitterly persecuted and many were killed but the movement continued to spread. Some of the Bahá'ís travelled from Írán and 'Iráq to Adrianople in the hope of seeing Bahá'u'lláh.

The Turkish authorities in Adrianople treated Bahá'u'lláh with great respect. This did not please the Iranian consul in the city. Mírzá Yaḥya and Siyyid Muhammad assisted the consul in his task of ensuring a further banishment for Bahá'u'lláh. They sent false accusations to the capital of the Ottoman Empire, Constantinople, accusing Bahá'u'lláh of plotting to overthrow the Ottoman regime.

The Governor of Adrianople, who held Bahá'u'lláh in great esteem, several times denied these accusations in writing but the central authorities eventually sent an order of banishment.

One morning, Bahá'u'lláh's house was surrounded by soldiers and the inhabitants of the city, Christian and Muslim, wept openly in the streets as the orders were read out. Several consuls of foreign powers resident in Adrianople offered to intercede on behalf of the exiles but Bahá'u'lláh declined these offers of help.

Recent aerial photograph of the Old City of 'Akká looking southward. The citadel where Bahá'u'lláh was imprisoned is in the centre foreground

Banishment to the Holy Land

Soldiers escorted the exiles from Adrianople to Gallipoli. No one knew their final destination or what was planned for them. At Gallipoli orders were issued that Bahá'u'lláh and his followers, together with a few of the followers of Mírzá Yahyá, were to be sent to prison in 'Akká, while four of Bahá'u'lláh's followers were to go to Cyprus with Mírzá Yahyá and his companions. As they left Gallipoli Bahá'u'lláh warned his followers that the journey ahead of them would be worse than anything that they had yet encountered. He advised anyone who did not feel strong enough to face it to leave at once, as they would be unable to leave later. No one left.

'Akká was a penal colony in a remote corner of the Ottoman Empire. The worst criminals from all parts of the Empire were sent there. The water and air of 'Akká were foul and the place was overrun with vermin and full of disease. It was said of 'Akká that if a bird flew over the city, so putrid was the air that it would fall down dead.

The sea journey to 'Akká was one of miserable discomfort. At Haifa, Mírzá Yahyá and his companions in exile left the main party.

On arrival at 'Akká, on 31 August 1868, the exiles were met by a hostile crowd of townspeople who had been told that the Bahá'is were the vilest and most despicable criminals. The crowd hurled stones and insults and spat on the prisoners.

The edict of perpetual banishment imposed on Bahá'u'lláh and his followers was read aloud from the steps of the mosque as a warning to the townspeople to have nothing to do with the prisoners. The order was one of strict imprisonment. The Bahá'is were forbidden to associate with each other or with the townspeople. Bahá'u'lláh himself was confined in a mud-floored cell that was open to wind and rain while the rest of the party were crowded into a few rooms nearby. On the first night in prison they were given no food or drink. All except two fell ill with malaria and dysentery and three died.

The Bahá'is in Írán and elsewhere did not know where Bahá'u'lláh was or even if he was still alive. When news reached them, some set out on foot for the prison city. At first they could not get into the city but stood for hours and sometimes days beyond the second moat in the hope of glimpsing Bahá'u'lláh at the cell window. Some brought plants with them, refusing to drink the little water they carried across the desert and saving it for the plants. They made a garden with these flowers outside the city.

Mírzá Mihdí, Bahá'u'lláh's second son, fell through an unguarded skylight in the prison roof and died as a result of the injuries he sustained. His last request to his father was that his own life might be accepted as a ransom for those who were unable to get access into the prison. A few months later the prison accommodation was needed by the Turkish army. The exiles were moved out into a house in the city where they were kept in very crowded conditions.

Gradually however, the changes that had taken place in Baghdád, Constantinople and Adrianople began to occur in 'Akká. The prison governor, the officials of the town and the townspeople began to recognize Bahá'u'lláh's innocence and his exceptional qualities. 'Abdu'l-Bahá, Bahá'u'lláh's eldest son, who took upon himself the work of Bahá'u'lláh's household affairs, was a loved and respected figure. The governor of the prison sent his own son to 'Abdu'l-Bahá for his education. This governor wished to render some act of service for Bahá'u'lláh, who suggested that he rebuild the town aqueduct which had been in disrepair for thirty years. When Bahá'u'lláh had been nine years in the city the edict of perpetual banishment was completely ignored by the prison governor and the officials. 'Abdu'l-Bahá rented a pleasant house outside the city for his Father, and Bahá'u'lláh, who had not seen trees and flowers growing for nine years, moved out of the city. Two years later, a spacious mansion which had just been completed at Bahjí was rented by 'Abdu'l-Bahá and it was in that mansion that Bahá'u'lláh spent the last thirteen years of His earthly life.

With the day-to-day administration of affairs in 'Abdu'l-Bahá's hands, Bahá'u'lláh was free to devote his time to writing. He rarely gave personal interviews but his influence was widely felt and the rulers of Palestine envied his power and influence.

Professor E. G. Browne, a distinguished Orientalist from Cambridge, spent five days at Bahjí and has left this account of an interview with Bahá'u'lláh.

In the corner, where the divan met the wall sat a wondrous and venerable figure.... The face of him on whom I gazed I can never forget, though I cannot describe it. Those piercing eyes seemed to read one's very soul; power and authority sat on that ample brow; while the deep lines on the forehead and face implied an age which the jet-black hair and beard flowing down in indistinguishable luxuriance almost to the waist seemed to belie. No need to ask in whose presence I stood, as I bowed myself before one who is the object of a devotion and love which kings might envy and emperors sigh for in vain!

A mild dignified voice bade me be seated, and then continued: *'Praise be to God that thou has attained!... Thou hast come to see a prisoner and an exile... We desire but the good of the world and the happiness of the nations; yet they deem us a stirrer-up of strife and sedition worthy of bondage and banishment... That all nations should become one in faith and all men as brothers; that the bonds of affection and unity between the sons of men should be strengthened; that diversity of religion should cease, and differences of race be annulled— what harm is there in this?... Yet so it shall be; these fruitless strifes, these ruinous wars shall pass away, and the 'Most Great Peace' shall come... Do not you in Europe need this also? Is not this that which Christ foretold?... Yet do we see your kings and rulers lavishing their treasures more freely on means for the destruction of the Human race than on that which would conduce to the happiness of mankind... These strifes and this bloodshed and discord must cease, and all men be as one*

Shrine of the Báb on Mount Carmel, Haifa, Israel

*kindred and one family... Let not a man glory in this, that he
loves his country; let him rather glory in this, that he loves his
kind.'*[21]

Bahá'u'lláh visited Haifa four times in the last years of his life and
pitched his tent on Mount Carmel. He pointed out to 'Abdu'l-Bahá
a piece of land on the rocky hillside where the remains of the Báb
should be buried. There are gardens on the hillside now, green lawns
and avenues of shady cypresses surrounding a beautiful building of
white marble under which the remains of the Báb and his young
companion were laid to rest.

Door to the Shrine of Bahá'u'lláh, Bahjí

On 29 May 1892, Bahá'u'lláh's earthly life ended. The bells of 'Akká which, twenty-four years earlier, had warned the people of the coming of the exile, tolled out his passing and a multitude of people walked out to the mansion at Bahjí and wept bitterly. There was a week of mourning during which the notables and government officials paid their respects. A telegram was sent to the Sultan of the Ottoman Empire which read 'The Sun of Bahá has set'.

As Shoghi Effendi wrote in his survey of the first hundred years of Bahá'í history, 'With the ascension of Bahá'u'lláh draws to a close a period which, in many ways, is unparalleled in the world's religious history... An epoch, unsurpassed in its sublimity, its fecundity and duration by any previous Dispensation... had terminated'.[22]

'Abdu'l-Bahá

'Abdu'l-Bahá, the eldest son of Bahá'u'lláh, was born on the night of 23 May 1844, the same night on which the Báb declared his mission to Mullá Ḥusayn. He was eight when Bahá'u'lláh was imprisoned in Ṭihran. A mob sacked the family home and they were forced into hiding for a time. 'Abdu'l-Bahá accompanied his parents into exile and he recognized his father's station ten years before Bahá'u'lláh made his declaration in the Garden of Riḍván. 'Abdu'l-Bahá was thus the first person to believe in the mission of Bahá'u'lláh. He was nine at the time.

When Bahá'u'lláh left Baghdád for the mountains of Kurdistan, 'Abdu'l-Bahá's grief was intense. He spent much of the two years that Bahá'u'lláh was away copying and memorizing the writings of the Báb. He was overjoyed at his father's return and from that time onwards he was Bahá'u'lláh's closest companion. He never received a formal education but learnt all that he knew from Bahá'u'lláh. He was an active, happy person. He inherited his parents' love of nature and the countryside. His favourite sport was horse riding.

On the journey from 'Iráq to Constantinople, 'Abdu'l-Bahá supervised the feeding and accommodation of the entire party of exiles. At night he guarded his father's carriage. In Adrianople he

Bahá'í gardens surrounding the Mansion at Bahjí

gradually took over the day-to-day administration of Bahá'u'lláh's affairs. He began to be known as 'The Master', a title given him by Bahá'u'lláh, though after the passing of Bahá'u'lláh he referred to himself simply as 'Abdu'l-Bahá, the servant of Bahá. He shielded his Father from those who were merely curious visitors but recognized with an extraordinary insight those who were seeking truth. He was loved by very many and respected even by those who wished him ill. He was gentle, couteous, forgiving, generous and unfailingly kind.

In 'Akká he married Munírih Khánum, the daughter of two early followers of the Báb. The marriage was a very happy one but of the nine children born, five died.

As soon as the restrictions on the prisoners began to be relaxed, 'Abdu'l-Bahá became a familiar figure in the mean and crowded streets of 'Akká. He helped everyone he could, regardless of their colour, creed and background. He went to the poorest homes where he washed and comforted the sick. His own wants were very few. He lived simply and dressed inexpensively but his appearance was always spotless. He worked early and late and spent a large part of each night in prayer and meditation. He loved children, and loved to give presents and to make people happy. 'My home', he said, 'is the home of laughter and mirth'.

After the Bahá'u'lláh's passing from this life, his written Will and Testament was read out to his family. 'Abdu'l-Bahá was appointed by Bahá'u'lláh as the Head of the Bahá'í Faith and as the only authoritative interpreter of the Bahá'í teachings. He called on all the Baha'ís to turn to and obey 'Abdu'l-Bahá. Despite this clear directive, some of Bahá'u'lláh's own family, motivated by envy and jealousy, refused to do this. They worked steadily to destroy 'Abdu'l-Bahá's authority. As a result of their activities, 'Abdu'l-Baha spent the years from 1901–08 once again in strict confinement in 'Akká. In 1904 and 1907 two commissions were appointed by the Ottoman authorities to enquire into charges made against him. False evidence was supplied to both commissions by corrupt witnesses and in 1907 his exile or execution was about to be recommended to the Sultan when the revolt of the Young Turks caused a change of regime in the Ottoman Empire. All political and religious prisoners of the Ottomans were set free.

During these years of trouble and difficulty, 'Abdu'l-Bahá worked steadily on. He looked after the hungry and sick people in 'Akká and he kept up an enormous correspondence with Bahá'ís in many

The holy Tomb of the Báb and 'Abdu'l-Bahá in Haifa from an original line drawing

countries. In the face of persistent attacks by his own relatives, he
constructed a simple stone shrine on Mount Carmel on the exact site
pointed out to him by Bahá'u'lláh as the final resting place for the
remains of the martyred Báb.

As soon as he was freed from prison, 'Abdu'l-Bahá began to plan
a journey to Europe and America. Poor health delayed his
immediate departure but in August 1911 he started on his journey to
the West. He was then in his late sixties and had spent nearly sixty
years in exile, some in prison, living continually with persecution
and hardship.

In September 1911 'Abdu'l-Bahá arrived in Britain and his first
public address in the West was given at the City Temple church in
London.

During the next two years he travelled in Europe and America spreading the Bahá'í teachings with the utmost wisdom and with complete devotion. Much of his time was spent in giving addresses and receiving visitors. He travelled cheaply avoiding all ostentation and unnecessary expense. In the United States he went from coast to coast and delivered more than 140 addresses in that country and Canada.

'Abdu'l-Bahá returned to Haifa in 1913. When the First World War broke out, he was once again a prisoner of the Turkish authorities. During the four years of isolation and danger, 'Abdu'l-Bahá began to organize an intensive agricultural operation near Tiberias in order to grow wheat for the people of Palestine. He continued his serene life of prayer and charity to all. As the war ended, his own life and and those of his immediate family were in grave danger. The Turkish authorities threatened to crucify 'Abdu'l-Bahá and his family on the slopes of Mount Carmel. When news of this threat reached London, General Allenby was ordered to extend every protection and consideration to 'Abdu'l-Bahá'. He took Haifa several days before it was believed possible for him to do so and his cable to London read: 'Have today taken Palestine. Notify the world that 'Abdu'l-Bahá is safe.' After the war was over, the British goverment conferred a knighthood upon 'Abdu'l-Bahá, in recognition of his work for the peace and prosperity of the area. He accepted the honour but never used the title.

On 28 November 1921, 'Abdu'l-Bahá passed away in Haifa. Up to the last few days of his life, he lived and worked as he had always done, with no thought for his own rest or comfort. At his funeral, Jews, Muslims and Christians paid tribute to him and mourned with the Bahá'ís their great loss in his passing.

'Abdu'l-Bahá's unique position

'Abdu'l-Bahá occupies a unique position unknown in any previous religion. While his station was essentially a human one, he was at the same time the Perfect Exemplar of the Bahá'í teachings and was endowed with superhuman knowledge. As the appointed successor to Bahá'u'lláh he was as a stainless mirror reflecting to men the light of the Manifestation of God. Under his continuous and specific instructions, the unity of the Bahá'ís was preserved and the Bahá'ís began to build an administrative order in accordance with the outline drawn up by Bahá'u'lláh. In his many letters and addresses he explained more fully the general principles drawn up by

'Abdu'l-Bahá in Paris, 1912

Bahá'u'lláh and their application in the world. His daily life was a proof that it is possible for a human being to live a life of complete devotion to God and service to humanity under the most difficult conditions.

Growth of the Bahá'í Faith during the lifetimes of its three central figures
During the ministry of the Báb (1844–50) his Faith had reached only Persia and 'Iráq, but from 1853 to 1892, the ministry of Bahá'u'lláh, the Bahá'í Faith was taken to thirteen other countries. The Báb and Bahá'u'lláh are the twin founders of this new world religion, but due to the special position of 'Abdu'l-Bahá as the 'Exemplar' and the 'Centre of the Covenant', his writings also form part of the Bahá'í Scripture. From the time Bahá'u'lláh passed away

37

until the death of 'Abdu'l-Bahá, the Faith spread to another twenty-two countries, raising the total to thirty-seven by the end of 1921. Even at that early date, with the Faith not even eighty years old, it could be classed as a world religion as the countries opened included China, Burma, Australia, Russia, eight European and three African countries, Brazil, Canada and the United States of America.

A Tablet of 'Abdu'l-Bahá

Know thou of a certainty that Love is the secret of God's holy Dispensation, the manifestation of the All-Merciful, the fountain of spiritual outpourings. Love is heaven's kindly light, the Holy Spirit's eternal breath that vivifieth the human soul. Love is the cause of God's revelation unto man, the vital bond inherent, in accordance with the divine creation, in the realities of things. Love is the one means that ensureth true felicity both in this world and the next. Love is the light that guideth in darkness, the living link that uniteth God with man, that assureth the progress of every illumined soul. Love is the most great law that ruleth this mighty and heavenly cycle, the unique power that bindeth together the divers elements of this material world, the supreme magnetic force that directeth the movements of the spheres in the celestial realms. Love revealeth with unfailing and limitless power the mysteries latent in the universe. Love is the spirit of life unto the adorned body of mankind, the establisher of true civilization in this mortal world, and the shedder of imperishable glory upon every high-aiming race and nation.

Whatsoever people is graciously favoured therewith by God, its name shall surely be magnified and extolled by the Concourse from on high, by the company of angels, and the denizens of the Abhá Kingdom. And whatsoever people turneth its heart away from this Divine Love—the revelation of the Merciful—shall err grievously, shall fall into despair, and be utterly destroyed. That people shall be denied all refuge, shall become even as the vilest creatures of the earth, victims of degradation and shame.

O ye beloved of the Lord! Strive to become the manifestations of the love of God, the lamps of divine guidance shining amongst the kindreds of the earth with the light of love and concord.

All hail to the revealers of this glorious light![23]

2 WHAT BAHÁ'ÍS BELIEVE

The oneness of humanity

'There can be no doubt whatever that the people of the world, of whatever race or religion, derive their inspiration from one heavenly Source, and are the subjects of one God'.[24]

(Bahá'u'lláh)

'All men are the leaves and fruit of one same tree... they all have the same origin. The same rain has fallen upon them all, the same sun makes them grow, they are all refreshed by the same breeze... the whole of humanity is enveloped by the Mercy and Grace of God. As the Holy Writings tell us: All men are equal before God. He is no respecter of persons'.[25]

('Abdu'l-Bahá)

The principle of the oneness of humanity is the pivot of Bahá'u'lláh's teachings. He explains that humanity has evolved socially through different stages of development just as an individual human body has evolved physically through different stages of growth. In early times men lived in isolated family groups, these family groups evolved into tribal units, later on these tribal units evolved into city states and finally into nations. World unity, Bahá'u'lláh teaches, is the last stage in the evolution of humanity towards maturity.

The purpose of his coming to earth, Bahá'u'lláh explains, was to enable men to become united. He wrote: *'We verily, have come to unite and weld together all that dwell on earth'.*[26]

His teachings, he says, are for every person living on the planet, for world unity involves everyone and no soul must be left out. The unity towards which men are evolving is not a dull uniformity but a unity in diversity, for in the Bahá'í teachings every group of people can find the highest possible expression of their own particular ideals and aspirations. At the same time, every group or nation can share in the heritage and achievements of all the others. *'The Glory of Humanity'*, 'Abdu'l-Bahá wrote, *'is the heritage of each one.'*[27]

World unity will be built upon individual recognition of this oneness of humanity as the central spiritual principle of life today. The unity will not be imposed from above by any powerful group but will evolve gradually in human consciousness, until men everywhere realize that *'the world is but one country and mankind its citizens'.*[28] (Bahá'u'lláh). This change in consciousness will lead to an organic change in society such as the world has not yet experienced. The world civilization which will evolve will be of a richness and diversity that men can hardly at present imagine.

Bahá'u'lláh has brought specific guidance for humanity to enable the world to pass from disunity to unity.

'O contending peoples and kindreds of the earth! Set your faces towards unity, and let the radiance of its light shine upon you'.[29] *'Be ye as the fingers of one hand, the members of one body.'*[30]

'He who is your Lord, the All-Merciful, cherisheth in his heart the desire of beholding the entire human race as one soul and one body.'[31]

The oneness of religion

The gift of God to this enlightened age is the knowledge of the oneness of mankind and of the fundamental oneness of religion.[32] ('Abdu'l-Bahá)

Bahá'is believe that all the great religions of the world are divine in origin. They have all been revealed by God to men in different places and different ages according to the evolving needs and capacities of the people. No age has ever been without guidance from God and as long as there are men on earth, God will give them guidance.

God himself is above and beyond human understanding. His guidance is given to men through his messengers, perfect and stainless souls who are referred to as manifestations of God. The manifestations of God are not God themselves but they are like perfect mirrors reflecting the light of God to men. They are like the rays of the sun which transmit the light of the sun to earth; they are intermediaries between God and humanity. They reflect, in their lives and teachings, the perfections of God. Through these manifestations, God causes man to know and love him. Knowledge of God is only possible for man through these manifestations, and the knowledge of their perfections is the fullest knowledge of God to which finite minds can attain.

As a token of his mercy... and as a proof of his loving-kindness, he hath manifested unto men the Day Stars of his divine guidance, the Symbols of his divine unity, and hath ordained the knowledge of these sanctified Beings to be identical with the knowledge of his own self.[33] (Bahá'u'lláh)

The appearance of a manifestation of God on earth is so rare an event in human history that we only have the names of a few: Krishna, Abraham, Zoroaster, Moses, Buddha, Jesus, Muḥammad, the Báb, Bahá'u'lláh. Each one of them has founded a religion and inspired a civilization. Each one was bitterly opposed, ridiculed, scorned and ill-treated by the people among whom they first appeared. Only a few of their contemporaries recognized their station. Gradually, other men grew to recognize them. After their life on earth was over, they were and still are loved, revered and followed by millions. Alone and unaided by any earthly power, they established their sovereignty over the hearts of men. They are the true educators of humanity whose purpose is to draw men ever nearer to God and to assist in the advancement of human civilization.

Bahá'u'lláh has explained clearly the dual station of the manifestations of God which past ages have found so confusing. Each manifestation has a divine station. Each and every one has been endowed with all the attributes of God. They can therefore be regarded as one soul and the same person.

If thou wilt observe with discriminating eyes, thou wilt behold them all abiding in the same tabernacle, soaring in the same heaven, seated upon the same throne, uttering the same speech, and proclaiming the same Faith. Such is the unity of those Essences of Being.[34]

At the same time, each manifestation has a distinct individuality and appears in this world as a human person, different in appearance, background and personality to any that have lived on earth before. Each time such a manifestation appears on earth, it is as if the spirit of all the former manifestations return with him. He builds on what the previous manifestations have taught, brings a new message which is particularly appropriate to the age in which he appears and looks forward to the coming of the next manifestation.

As they appear as men among other men, mankind is able to

exercise free will in choosing whether or not to recognize the manifestation of God for each age.

Bahá'ís therefore revere all the founders of the world's religions and regard the scriptures of all the world's religions as sacred.

Bahá'u'lláh, Bahá'ís believe, is the latest of these messengers to appear on earth. He explains that every religion is made up of two parts, the spiritual teachings and the social teachings. On the higher spiritual level there is a wonderful harmony between all the great religions. The differences exist at a social level and are about religious practices, laws and observances. Bahá'u'lláh explains that the social aspects of religion are not eternal and unchanging but that they change in every age according to the needs of the people.

Differences also arise within and between different religions, as a result of man-made additions to the original teachings. The purity of the message becomes distorted by the followers. It is for this reason that God sends another messenger to renew and develop the spiritual message previously given. The outward, material aspects of every religion go through stages of birth, growth and decay. When the period of decay is reached, a new seed is planted in the hearts of men by a new messenger and a new growth begins.

Bahá'u'lláh's mission is to bring about unity among the religions of the world. Religion, he teaches, is the foremost agency for the peace and orderly progress of the world. World peace will involve a world-wide renewal of religion.

Elimination of Prejudice

Prejudice, whether of religion, race, class, nation and colour has been and still is the most fertile cause of war; all the divisions, hatred and warfare in the world are caused by one or other of these prejudices. The true remedy for such prejudices is the consciousness of the oneness of mankind. Once a person has gained a spiritual awareness of the unity of mankind, he can overcome his own personal prejudices.

Bahá'u'lláh tells us that we should regard the different races and and nations with the eye of oneness:

Verily the words which have descended from the heaven of the Will of God are the source of unity and harmony for the world. Close your eyes to racial differences, and welcome all with the light of oneness. We desire but the good of the world and the happiness of the nations, that all nations should become one in faith and all men as brothers; that the bonds of affection and unity between the sons of men should be strengthened; that diversity of religion should cease, and differences of race by annulled.[35]

'Abdu'l-Bahá wrote:

In the estimation of God, there is no distinction of colour; all are one in colour and beauty of servitude to him. Colour is not important; the heart is all-important. It mattereth not what the exterior may be if the heart is pure and white within. God doth not behold differences of hue and complexion. He looketh at the hearts. He whose morals and virtues are praiseworthy is preferred in the presence of God; he who is devoted to the Kingdom is most beloved. In the realm of genesis and creation the question of colour is of least importance.[36]
    Consider the flowers of a garden; though differing in kind, colour, form and shape, yet, inasmuch as they are refreshed by the waters of one spring, revived by the breath of one wind, invigorated by the rays of one sun, this diversity increaseth their charm, and addeth unto their beauty.[37]

Harmony of religion and science
Bahá'u'lláh teaches that religion and science are in harmony with one another. True religion and true science have never contradicted each other. They are complementary aspects of one truth.
    Both are progressive. Religion is gradually revealed to man by God. Man gradually discovers the mysteries of science through his own powers of investigation. Both forces are needed by man. Religion is the aid he needs for his spiritual growth. Science is the means by which he can advance materially. Religion and science are described by Bahá'u'lláh as the two most potent forces in the world of existence.
Religion and science are the two wings upon which man's intelligence can soar into the heights, with which the human soul can progress. It is not possible to fly with one wing alone. Should a man try to fly with the wing of religion alone he would quickly fall in the quagmire of superstition, whilst on the other hand, with the wing of science alone he would also make no progress, but fall into the despairing slough of materialism.[38] ('Abdu'l-Bahá)

A Bahá'í music group outside an exhibition tent

True civilization will become a reality on earth when men realize their need for both science and religion. Both the founders of religions and the pioneers of science have suffered scorn and denial from their contemporaries. Conflict has arisen among their followers as a result of human error usually caused by ignorance and prejudice. *'Religion and science walk hand in hand, and any religion contrary to science is not the truth.'*[39] ('Abdu'l-Bahá)

It is interesting, in the light of the Bahá'í teachings, to find that the most recent advances in science emphasize the oneness of the entire universe and the interdependence of all created things.

44

Independent investigation into truth

Bahá'u'lláh does not wish anyone to accept his revelation blindly. He asks each individual to look into it for himself, to use his own eyes and ears, his own faculty of reasoning and to make up his own mind.

This is the first time in human history that the independent search for truth has been a practical possibility. As more people learn to read and write, they will be able to decide for themselves about the truth or falsity of Bahá'u'lláh's claim. It will no longer be necessary, as it has been in the past, for a certain group of people to present the religion to the rest.

Genuine independent investigation demands of men much more than a blind acceptance of a faith taught by someone else. Bahá'u'lláh explains that each person must detach himself from inherited belief and prejudice. He must abandon at the outset the idea that he is right and everyone else is wrong.

> ... when you meet those whose opinions differ from your own, do not turn away your face from them. All are seeking truth, and there are many roads leading thereto... Do not allow differences of opinion, or diversity of thought, to separate you from your fellow-men, or to be the cause of dispute... Rather, search diligently for the truth and make all men your friends. [40]
> ('Abdu'l-Bahá)

A genuine search for truth by all men will lead to unity. *'Truth is one in all the religions and by means of it the unity of the world can be realized... If only men would search out truth, they would find themselves united.'* [41]

The nature of God

Bahá'u'lláh teaches that man's finite mind will never understand God, for the finite cannot comprehend the infinite. It is like expecting a table to have an intellectual understanding of the mind of the carpenter who made it. 'Abdu'l-Bahá wrote:

> ... man cannot grasp the Essence of Divinity, but can, by his reasoning power, by observation, by his intuitive faculties and the revealing power of his faith, believe in God, discover the bounties of His Grace. [42]

While men cannot understand the essential nature of God, they can be certain that the divine reality exists:

Regard thou the one true God as One who is apart from, and immeasurably exalted above, all created things. The whole universe reflecteth his glory, while he is himself independent of, and transcendeth his creatures. This is the true meaning of Divine unity. He who is the Eternal Truth is the one Power who exerciseth undisputed sovereignty over the world of being, whose image is reflected in the mirror of the entire creation. All existence is dependent upon him, and from him is derived the source of the sustenance of all things...[43] (Bahá'u'lláh)

God is to be regarded as the fashioner of the universe. He is, at the same time, a personal, loving father to every human being who has ever lived and will ever live. The combination of these two roles is almost beyond the grasp of man, but this is what has been taught by the founder of every religion. Each one has extolled the greatness of God and each one has taught that God has a purpose and a great love for every human being. These founders of religion, the manifestations, are the link between God and man. Bahá'u'lláh refers to them as:

...luminous Gems of Holiness which appear out of the realm of the spirit, in the noble form of the human temple, made manifest unto all men, that they may impart unto the world the mysteries of the unchangeable Being, and tell of the subtleties of his imperishable Essence.[44]

Man can learn more of God and draw nearer to him by turning to these manifestations.
Bahá'u'lláh wrote:

So perfect and comprehensive is his creation that no mind nor heart, however keen or pure, can ever grasp the nature of the most insignificant of his creatures; much less fathom the mystery of him who is the Day Star of Truth, Who is the invisible and unknowable Essence. The conceptions of the devoutest of mystics, the attainments of the most accomplished among men, the highest praise which human tongue or pen can render are all the product of man's finite mind and are conditioned by its limitations... From time immemorial he hath been veiled in the ineffable sanctity of his exalted self, and will everlastingly continue to be wrapped in the impenetrable mystery of his unknowable Essence. Every attempt to attain to an understanding of his inaccessible reality hath ended in complete bewilderment, and every effort to approach his exalted self and envisage his Essence hath resulted in hopelessness and failure.[45]

The nature of man

The human species is a higher form of life than the mineral, vegetable and animal creation. God has given man reason and intellect. He has also given man a soul capable of knowing and loving God.

O Son of Man! I loved thy creation, hence I created thee. Wherefore, do thou love me, that I may name thy name and fill thy soul with the spirit of life.[46] (Bahá' u' lláh)

From everything that he has created, God has singled out for his special favour the pure, the gem-like reality of man, and invested it with a unique capacity of knowing him and of reflecting the greatness of His glory.[47] (Bahá' u' lláh)

Man has the capacity, by turning to a manifestation of God, to attain the qualities and attributes that are of God: love, truth, mercy, justice.

Every man has free will to decide whether or not he will turn to the teachings of God. All men are equal in the sight of God but each soul is a unique creation with different abilities and capacities. All that man might potentially achieve, he will only achieve by his own efforts.

Each human being has a spiritual higher nature which he must develop in order to know and love God. Each also has a physical, animal nature. Bahá' u' lláh teaches that man's body should be the willing servant of the soul. Man's greatest happiness lies in spiritual, not physical contentment.

The soul of man, life and death

The soul, being a spiritual and not a physical reality, is not destroyed when the human body dies. The soul is connected with the body during man's life on earth in the way that a light is reflected in a mirror. Should the mirror be destroyed, the light will continue to shine.

Each soul comes into existence at conception and is a unique creation. Physical existence on earth is a necessary experience for almost every soul. It is a stage of existence when a human being has the chance to develop his own spiritual capacities, such as being truthful, compassionate, loving and generous. We shall need these qualities after our physical existence so they are developing here on this earth in the same way that a child develops in the womb its eyes, ears, nose, hands and legs. The child in the womb does not yet use them but its future existence will be very limited without them.

The existence of the soul after death is as different from the life we know as the life of a child in its mother's womb is different from its life outside the womb after it is born. The soul, freed from the body much in the way that a captured bird is freed from a cage, will continue to progress and advance towards God. Our progress in the next world will depend on the efforts that we have made here.

'Heaven' and 'Hell' are not places but states of being, Heaven is nearness to God and Hell remoteness from him. These states of being exist in this life as well as the life beyond. In the same way, life and death as spoken of in the scriptures, refer to a man's spiritual life or lack of it.

The death of the body is not something to be feared but welcomed as a birth into a fuller life.

O Son of the Supreme! I have made death a messenger of joy to thee. Wherefore dost thou grieve? I made the light to shed on thee its splendour. Why dost thou veil thyself therefrom?[48]

Know thou of a truth that the soul, after its separation from the body, will continue to progress until it attaineth the presence of God, in a state and condition which neither the revolution of ages and centuries, nor the changes and chances of this world, can alter. It will endure as long as the Kingdom of God, his sovereignty, his dominion and power will endure. It will manifest the signs of God and his attributes, and will reveal his long kindness and bounty... Blessed is the soul which, at the hour of its separation from the body, is sanctified from the vain imaginings of the people of the world. Such a soul liveth and moveth in accordance with the Will of its Creator, and entereth the all-highest Paradise... If any man be told that which hath been ordained for such a soul in the worlds of God... his whole being will instantly blaze out in his great longing to attain that most exalted, that sanctified and resplendent station . . .[49] (Bahá' u 'lláh)

Artist's model for the Temple of India. The design is based on the lotus flower. Work began in 1979

Evolution

Man is a distinct species. Like other forms of life, the vegetable and animal, man's physical form has evolved through different stages of development. At various times in his history, man has looked like an amoeba, a fish or an ape, but these outward appearances are not a proof that he is descended from any one of these.

The human species has developed over the centuries and millenia in much the same way that the embryo of a child develops in its mother's womb. A human person, from embryo to maturity, goes through many different stages, forms and appearances, yet its essential nature, that of a human, remains unchanged.

Good and evil

Bahá'u'lláh explained that there is only one force in the universe, the benevolent power of the one All-Powerful God whose love and goodness are infinite. It therefore follows that evil, where it can be seen, is not a positive thing in itself but is the absence or the lesser degree of good. Evil is the absence of good in the same way that darkness is the absence of light.

If a man acts in an evil way, this is because his lower, animal nature is more developed than his higher, spiritual nature. The remedy is for that person, with the assistance of others, to develop his higher nature.

All men have desires. They can be observed in the smallest children. Desire is a praiseworthy quality if directed towards the good of that individual and the rest of humanity. Desire is to ask for something more, it is an impulse that God has given man so that he may strive to acquire knowledge, to acquire perfections of character and draw nearer to God.

Good is found in obedience to God's commands; evil is when man knowingly turns away from him. While Bahá'u'lláh gives strength, courage, and purpose to man and emphasizes the merciful and forgiving nature of God, it still is made clear that man cannot escape his individual responsibility for using or misusing the powers and talents God has given to him.

Know thou that all men have been created in the nature made by God, the Guardian, the Self-Subsisting. Unto each one hath been prescribed a pre-ordained measure, as decreed in God's mighty and guarded Tablets. All that which ye potentially possess can, however, be manifested only as a result of your own volition. Your own acts testify to this truth . . . Men, however, have wittingly broken his law. Is such a behaviour to be attributed to God, or to their proper selves? Be fair in your judgment. Every good thing is of God, and every evil thing is from yourselves. [50] (Bahá'u'lláh)

How an individual should live

Behaviour

A Bahá'í should be known by his deeds rather than by his words.
The qualities that Bahá'u'lláh stresses are those given emphasis in all the major religions. An individual should strive to be honest, loving, courteous forgiving and generous. He should honour his parents, be hospitable and faithful. He should accept God's Will with a happy heart.

Bahá'u'lláh does not approve of asceticism but says that men should enjoy those good things of life that God has given them.

The path of God may lead through material poverty or through great wealth and possessions. Bahá'u'lláh advises his followers not to be troubled by poverty nor confident in riches. The greatest blessing man can have is a tranquil heart and this can only be attained by living in accord with the divine teachings.

Prayer and Fasting

PRAYER

Prayer is absolutely necessary for man's spiritual growth. Food helps his body to grow, prayer feeds his spirit. Bahá'u'lláh has made a daily prayer obligatory for all Bahá'ís but they may choose a long prayer, one of medium length or a short one.

Prayer is much more than a mere reciting of words. It involves our whole attitude, to life, thankfulness and attentiveness. 'Abdu'l-Bahá told the Bahá'ís that he prayed that their lives might be beautiful prayers of praise and service. *'Know that nothing will benefit thee in this life save supplication and invocation unto God, service in his vineyard, and with a heart full of love, to be in constant servitude unto him.'* [51]

THE FAST

From 2nd to 20th March each year, Bahá'ís, between the ages of 15 and 70 who are in good health, do not eat or drink between the hours of sunrise and sunset. Those who are travelling are exempt from the Fast together with expectant and nursing mothers.

The Fast is a time of spiritual renewal. It is a time when Bahá'ís make an extra effort to correct lazy and harmful spiritual habits that may have developed during the year. When people do not have to spend time and thought preparing food and eating it they have more time to turn their thoughts of God and the purpose of the Fast is to draw men nearer to God.

Daily Study
Bahá'ís are encouraged to spend a little time at the beginning and end of each day in reading from the Bahá'í writings and in meditating on what they have read. They should do this to refresh and renew their minds, not to tire them. Bahá'u'lláh says that it is better to read a short passage with joy and gladness than a long one carelessly.

Service to humanity
If we love God and want to follow his teachings, we will serve our fellow men. Bahá'u'lláh gives the service of humanity great importance in his teachings. When our motive is pure and disinterested and founded in our love for God, then our actions in the service of our fellows is prayer, worship and unity with God.

Bahá'u'lláh teaches that men should regard their daily work as worship of God. Man is not made just to work but work is made for man. It should be some activity that will ennoble and exalt men, not degrade them. All men have a basic human right to work and all

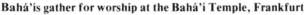

Bahá'ís gather for worship at the Bahá'í Temple, Frankfurt

should earn a living both with their hands and their heads, not just with one or the other. A man's work should not be drudgery or a necessary chore, but done in the spirit of service to humanity it is worship of God.

Teaching the Faith
There are no ministers or clergy in the Bahá'í Faith. Each Bahá'í is a Bahá'í teacher and each considers it a duty and privilege to spread the Bahá'í teachings. A Bahá'í teacher must have a firm belief in God and must strive to live up to the Bahá'í teachings. Bahá'u'lláh says that the best way to teach is to live by the teachings and thus teach by example. Where words are necessary, they should be used with the utmost wisdom. Bahá'ís are urged to share the teachings with all but if people do not wish to hear about them, to pray for them and leave them on their path to God.

Abstinence from drugs and alcohol
Bahá'u'lláh forbids the taking of intoxicating drinks and narcotics of any kind, except as remedies in cases of illness. He states that both can be harmful to the mind and body of man.

Obedience to governments
Bahá'ís must respect and abide by the laws of the land in which they live. Where changes in the law are necessary for the protection of human rights, these changes must be sought by non-violent means. As supporters of a world peace-keeping force, Bahá'ís are not pacifists but seek peaceful solutions wherever possible.

The newer patriotism
A Bahá'í is a world citizen. Patriotism is a natural human loyalty. There is nothing wrong with sane and intelligent patriotism but it is no longer sufficient in the twentieth century. A greater loyalty is now needed to the planet itself. This can only be developed through a spiritual awareness of the oneness and wholeness of the human race. *'It is not for him to pride himself who loveth his own country, but rather for him who loveth the whole world. The earth is but one country and mankind its citizens'.*[52] (Bahá'u'lláh)

The family
Happy and united families are the foundation stones of a harmonious and stable society. Monastic celibacy is forbidden to Bahá'ís and marriage is strongly encouraged but it is not obligatory.

In the Bahá'í Faith, marriage is exalted an an expression of God's purpose. *'And when he desired to manifest grace and beneficence to men, and to set the world in order, he revealed observances and created laws; among them he established the law of marriage, made it as a fortress for well-being and salvation . . .'*[53] (Bahá'u'lláh)

Marriage provides the best possible conditions for the spiritual and physical well-being of men and women. In this relationship they can best help each other to develop their full human potential, to grow spiritually and become self-sacrificing.

The primary purpose of marriage is stated to be the rearing of children. *'He saith, great is his glory; Marry, O people, that from you may appear he who will remember me amongst my servants; this is one of my commandments unto you; obey it as an assistance to yourself.'*[54] (Bahá'u'lláh)

As parenthood is the first and foremost duty for a husband and wife, it is this aspect of marriage which is perhaps most closely linked with fulfilling God's purpose for man. The most effective way of imparting to children an understanding of God's purpose for man is through example, so the goal is clear to Bahá'í parents.

Recognizing the love of God to be the true source of love among men, partners in marriage seek the support of their love for each other in their love of God. Happiness in marriage depends on it. *'Real love is impossible unless one turns his face towards God and be attracted to his Beauty.'*[55] ('Abdu'l-Bahá)

The fundamental qualities which link the soul with God—loyalty and faithfulness—must also become the foundation binding lovers in marriage. The most precious expression of this loyalty and faithfulness is chastity.

Briefly stated the Bahá'í conception of sex is based on the belief that chastity should be strictly practised by both sexes, not only because it is in itself highly commendable ethically, but also due to its being the only way to a happy and successful marital life. Sex relationships of any form, outside marriage, are not permissible therefore, and whosoever violates this rule will not only be responsible to God, but will incur the necessary punishment from society.

The Bahá'í Faith recognizes the value of the sex impulse, but condemns its illegitimate and improper expressions such as free love, companionate marriage and others, all of which it considers positively harmful to man and to the society in which he lives. The proper use of the sex instinct is the natural right of every individual, and it is precisely for this very purpose that the institution of marriage has been established. The Bahá'ís do not believe in the suppression of the sex impulse but in its regulation and control.[56] (Shoghi Effendi through his secretary)

Marriage is the foundation of a good family; good families in turn are the foundation of a stable civilization. *'Know thou that the command of marriage is eternal. It will never be changed nor altered. This is divine creation and there is not the slightest possibility that change or alteration affect this divine creation . . .'*[57] ('Abdu'l-Bahá)

The qualities of loyalty and faithfulness are vital in marriage. As sex relationships of any form outside marriage are not permissible, Bahá'ís are encouraged to marry while young. Divorce is possible for Bahá'ís but it is strongly condemned and is sought only as a last remedy when all attempts at reconciliation have failed.

A total of 43 friends attended the first conference of the Arctic and sub-Arctic regions of Europe, held in Torshavn, Faroe Islands, 1974

The arrangement of marriages by parents for their children is forbidden. Bahá'ís must choose their own marriage partners. Once they have made their choice, they must then seek parental approval. A Bahá'í marriage cannot take place unless the consent of all living natural parents is obtained. When the two families involved are united in their approval of a marriage, that marriage will have a better chance of success.

Bahá'ís are allowed to choose a marriage partner from any religious or racial background. As Bahá'ís regard the whole of mankind as one family, it is common to find marriages between persons of very different racial and cultural backgrounds. These marriages draw the families thus linked into ever wider circles of unity and thus promote the oneness of mankind.

A Bahá'í is not allowed to have more than one wife at a time but if a man becomes a Bahá'í when he already has a number of wives, he must continue to provide for them all and no new marriages may be contracted.

The third annual Bahá'í Children's Conference of Guyana was held in March 1977

The form of marriage service is extremely simple. The man and woman say to each other, before witnesses, '*We will all, verily, abide by the Will of God*'. The couple may choose music, prayers and readings to be used at the ceremony.

If the law of the land does not recognize Bahá'í marriage, a couple must have a civil marriage to be followed by the Bahá'í ceremony on the same day. If a Bahá'í marries a non-Bahá'í, the Bahá'í may participate in the religious marriage of the other providing he/she is not being committed to any laws of the other's faith. In England, Northern Ireland and Wales it is presently necessary to have a civil marriage as well as the Bahá'í marriage but since early 1978 a legal Bahá'í marriage may be performed in Scotland and Bahá'í Marriage Officers are recognised officially.

The rights of all members of the family must be respected while the unity of the family is sustained. The children have certain obligations to their parents just as the parents have certain obligations to their children. It is the duty of the parents, by example, to teach their children the love of God and of their fellow men. Bahá'u'lláh also says that it is the responsibility of the parents to make adequate provision for the teaching and education of their children. Should the State not make proper provision, and the parents are unable to do so, the community and friends should help.

Equality of men and women
The building of a true Bahá'í marriage is dependent on another of Bahá'u'lláh's principles, that of equality of men and women.

The equality of the sexes is for Bahá'ís a spiritual and moral principle essential for the development of a just World Order. Without the full utilization of the talents and qualities of both men and women, full economic and social development for humanity is impossible.

> *The world of humanity has two wings—one is women and the other men. Not until both wings are equally developed can the bird fly.*[58]
> *As long as women are prevented from attaining their highest possibilities, so long will men be unable to achieve the greatness which might be theirs.*[59]

Bahá'u'lláh stated that women should be educated to the same standard as men and that they should have equal rights with men in

57

A group of women and children participating in a Bahá'í Women's Conference in the Solomon Islands, February 1975

society. If there is not enough money in a family to educate both a son and daughter, the parents are advised to spend the money on the daughter's education, for she is the potential mother and teacher of a new generation.

Bahá'u'lláh stated that no one can prevent or delay equality for women. He also said that when women participate fully and equally in the affairs of the world, war will cease.

These changes will not come about unless women themselves make a great effort to develop their full potential. They will have to strive: *'to attain greater perfection, to be man's equal in every respect, to make progress in all in which she has been backward, so that man will be compelled to acknowledge her equality of capacity and attainment'.*[60] ('Abdu'l-Bahá)

In the following passage, 'Abdu'l-Bahá explains what will happen as women take their rightful place in society:

The world in the past has been ruled by force, and man has dominated over woman by reason of his more forceful and aggressive qualities both of body and mind. But the balance is already shifting; force is losing its dominance, and mental alertness, intuition, and the spiritual qualities of love and service, in which woman is strong, are gaining ascendancy.

Hence the new age will be an age less masculine and more permeated with the feminine ideals, or, to speak more exactly, will be an age in which the masculine and feminine elements of civilization will be more evenly balanced.[61]

Universal compulsory education

Another important principle of Bahá'u'lláh is that everyone should receive a basic education so that all men and women will be literate.

Knowledge is one of the greatest gifts of God to man and those who deprive themselves of an opportunity to gain knowledge will live a more limited life than their fellows. The knowledge that is worthy of humanity is the study of such arts, sciences, crafts and skills that will benefit men and improve the quality of life on earth.

Prejudice is often founded on ignorance and the spread of education will help to remove prejudices between people.

All people are different in capacity and ability. The education given to children should be such as to enable each child to achieve his full potential, and should encourage constructive cooperation among children.

Bahá'u'lláh has announced that inasmuch as ignorance and lack of education are barriers of separation among mankind, all must receive training and instruction. Through this provision the lack of mutual understanding will be remedied and the unity of mankind furthered and advanced. Universal education is a universal law.

The education of each child is compulsory . . . In addition to this widespread education each child must be taught a profession, art, or trade, so that every member of the community will be enabled to earn his own livelihood. Work done in the spirit of service is the highest form of worship.[62]
('Abdu'l-Bahá)

Unfolding of world civilization

Human society is evolving in the direction of world unity. We have already evolved small units, the family, the tribe, the city state, the nation. Each stage of development has been necessary and suitable for mankind. The next step is the creation of a peacefully united world commonwealth. The basis of such a unity must be a spiritual one but there are certain steps that the nations of the world can take which will assist in the peaceful evolution of a united world.

These are:

(a)   The elimination of extremes of wealth and poverty both within and between nations.

(b)   The establishment of an international auxiliary language. This language would be taught in all schools in addition to the children's mother tongue.

(c)   The development of a world commonwealth and parliament with just representation of all peoples.

(d)   The formation of a federal world government or world Super-State, a Supreme Tribunal and an International Executive adequate to enforce its authority on every recalcitrant member of the commonwealth and to safeguard the rights of all and to resist aggression.

(e)   The selection of a world script, a world literature and a uniform and universal system of currency, weights and measures to simplify and facilitate intercourse and understanding among the races and nations of mankind.

The Guardian of the Bahá'í Faith wrote in 1936:

In such a world society, science and religion, the two most potent forces in human life, will be reconciled, will cooperate, and will harmoniously develop. The press will, under such a system, while giving full scope to the expression of the diversified views and convictions of mankind, cease to be mischievously manipulated by vested interests, whether private or public, and will be liberated from the influence of contending governments and peoples. The economic resources of the world will be organized, its sources of raw materials will be tapped and fully utilized, its markets will be coordinated and developed, and the distribution of its products will be equitably regulated.

National rivalries, hatreds, and intrigues will cease, and racial animosity and prejudices will be replaced by racial amity, understanding and cooperation. The causes of religious strife will be permanently removed, economic barriers and restrictions will be completely abolished, and the inordinate distinction between classes will be obliterated. Destitution on the one hand, and gross accumulation of ownership on the other, will disappear. The enormous energy dissipated and wasted on war, whether economic or political, will be consecrated to such ends as will extend the range of human inventions and technical development, to the increase of the productivity of mankind, to the extermination of disease, to the extension of scientific research, to the raising of the standard of physical health, to the sharpening and refinement of the human brain, to the exploitation of the unused and unsuspected resources of the planet, to the prolongation of human life, and to the furtherance of any other agency that can stimulate the intellectual, the moral, and spiritual life of the entire human race.[63]

Prohibitions

In addition to the prohibitions to which reference has already been made—asceticism, priesthood, the taking of alcohol and habit-forming drugs, Bahá'u'lláh also prohibits adultery, arson, backbiting, begging, calumny, cremation, confession of sins, cruelty to animals, gambling, homosexuality, the kissing of hands, murder, slave trading, theft and professional celibacy. Not only did he bring laws for the New Age, but he also had to annul some laws and practices of other religions which prevented the unity of mankind or were a hindrance to the onward march of civilization.

In 1931, Shogi Effendi wrote:

The call of Bahá'u'lláh is primarily directed against all forms of provincialism, all insularities and prejudices. If long-cherished ideals and time-honoured institutions, if certain social assumptions and religious formulae have ceased to promote the welfare of the generality of mankind, if they no longer minister to the needs of a continually evolving humanity, let them be swept away and relegated to the limbo of obsolescent and forgotten doctrines. Why should these, in a world subject to the immutable law of change and decay, be exempt from the deterioration that must needs overtake every human institution? For legal standards, political and economic theories are solely designed to safeguard the interest of humanity as a whole, and not humanity to be crucified for the preservation of the integrity of any particular law or doctrine.[63]

3   How the Bahá'ís Live

Introduction

Bahá'ís do not wear any distinctive clothing nor do they come from any particular racial group so it may be thought that it is not immediately possible to distinguish one from any other member of society. Yet as this Faith continues to grow there appear many distinctive characteristics noticeable among its members. As individuals they should have a confidence and serenity which comes from being acutely aware of what is happening in the world around them and what their particular purpose is in life. They feel that they know, in practical terms, what God wishes them to do under any circumstances.

Though distressed with the suffering being experienced by the millions of the poor, the starving, the homeless, the diseased, the enslaved, the persecuted among the world's population, they are happy in the knowledge that God has shown mankind a way to remedy all these evils and they feel they can make a positive contribution in effecting that remedy. Their philosophy is a simple one.

Mankind, as a whole, has rejected the Word of God as a power to help, and individual men have thereby lost the ability to live in harmony with their fellow men. The best good that anyone can do therefore is to bring the Word of God back to man.

God has revealed His Word again in this age through Bahá'u'lláh; to bring the message of Bahá'u'lláh to the peoples of the world is, consequently, of the utmost importance. This is the simple purpose of life as seen by the Bahá'ís. Bahá'u'lláh has a healing message; let the people know. All men have critical faculties, let them use them in this most important field of investigation. The Faith of God is for everyone, free and without restriction. No one should be deprived of the opportunity to hear of it.

What people do when they hear is then between themselves and God; no pressure or coercion must be used. The quality of the life, the radiance of the spirit, the joy of association, should contribute to the attraction. If, however, this spreading of the Word of God to all mankind is of such importance and if there is no professional

The Bahá'í Temple, Kampala

clergy, no one paid solely to be a teacher of the Bahá'í Faith, the question arises as to how it can reach around the world without some planning and organization. It cannot, and in the Bahá'í Scripture itself there is the outline of a teaching programme to reach out to the whole world and an administrative system which provides the basic constitution, as it evolves, for the Kingdom of God on earth.

It is this Administrative Order, this system of government, which functions at local, national and international levels, derives its authority from Bahá'í Scripture and in which every Bahá'í the world over is free to participate, that constitutes one of the most distinctive features of Bahá'í life. The Administrative Order itself is unique in religious history and it will be dealt with more fully later in this book. It is important to remember, however, that although community administration and forms of government appear to be very political and far from spiritual, in the Bahá'í Faith it is all part of the religion, forms an essential part of Scripture, and cannot be separated from the more apparently spiritual parts of the Faith such as prayer, meditation, fasting, worship, right living and the like. Indeed all these have a part to play in the administration itself and participation in some of the Bahá'í administrative activities can give a deeply rewarding spiritual experience.

A view of Haifa, Israel at night, looking down towards the sea from the Bahá'í Gardens behind the Shrine of the Báb, seen in the foreground

A new World Order
The Bahá'í World Community
One of the most distinctive features of the life of any Bahá'í is his burning desire to share his Faith with anyone who wishes to investigate. The other unique feature is the Bahá'í Administrative Order which enables every Bahá'í man, woman and child to be part of a united, active, ever-expanding Bahá'í World Community, and as part of that Community, be directly involved in the local, national and global plans for teaching the Faith. To gain some idea then of how Bahá'ís live, it is necessary to examine the various components of this evolving Administrative Order.

Chapter 1 brought us to the end of the Heroic or Apostolic Age of the Faith of Bahá'u'lláh. Almost fifty years of Divine Revelation, and nearly thirty years of inspired interpretation had come to an end. Over 20,000 martyrs, described by Shoghi Effendi in his book *God Passes By* as 'a galaxy of God-intoxicated heroes', had given their lives in Persia and imparted 'in their turn an added impetus to the steadily gathering momentum of God's nascent Faith'. The Faith itself had, in stretching across the globe, reached thirty five countries.

In accordance with the terms of the Will and Testament of 'Abdu'l-Bahá, (written for the most part many years before his death), Shoghi Effendi Rabbani, 'Abdu'l-Bahá's eldest grandson, was appointed Guardian of the Bahá'í Faith. Shoghi Effendi was, when he thus became head of the Faith, a young student of 24 at Balliol College, Oxford, working hard to equip himself to be the translator of Bahá'í Scripture and completely unaware of the staggering role his Grandfather had planned for him. He was called back to Haifa where 'Abdu'l-Bahá had lived and had been buried. With the burial of Bahá'u'lláh in Bahjí near 'Akká, and the Báb and 'Abdu'l-Bahá sharing a shrine on Mount Carmel, Haifa, the Holy Land had become, for the Bahá'ís at least, the heart of the entire planet.

The Guardianship of Shoghi Effendi
With the establishment of the Guardianship and, many years later, the election of the Universal House of Justice—its Supreme Administrative body—the Spiritual as well as the Administrative centres of the Faith were, unlike those of most other world religions, in one and the same place. Also unique were the terms of 'Abdu'l-Bahá's Will which, by virtue of the power of divinely-guided

interpretation it gave to the Guardian, protected the Faith from the divisions and schisms which have dissipated the spiritual forces of earlier religions.

Under the Guardianship of Shoghi Effendi, the Faith gradually spread to more and more countries, Bahá'í literature was translated into many languages and a new world society began to emerge.

The groundwork for all the advances which have taken place in the Bahá'í world; the inspiration for the great spiritual crusades which achieved these successes; the development of the world-wide Administrative Order; the extension and beautification of the World Centre of the Bahá'í Faith in the Holy Land were largely due to the genius and dedication of Shoghi Effendi, the Guardian of the Bahá'í Faith. Much has been written about the life and achievements of Shoghi Effendi who worked himself to a relatively early death at the age of sixty in November 1957, but the most comprehensive study is the 450-page tribute, '*The Priceless Pearl*' written by his widow, Canadian born Amatu' l-Bahá Rúḥíyyih Khánum. It is far too early to assess fully the amazing contribution Shoghi Effendi made to world history, and very little is known about him in the non-Bahá'í world. Were his written English the only evidence of his genius it would suffice to astonish any sincere investigator.

His written work includes a 181,000-word history of the first Bahá'í century and his monumental published letters between them contributed another 300,000 words. In addition, many thousands of letters were written to individuals, groups, committees, and local and National Assemblies.

He also wrote extensively in Persian and Arabic and a total of almost 15,000 of his authenticated letters have been collected, studied and microfilmed. His superb translations from Persian and Arabic into English of Bahá'í literature must in all total over three-quarters of a million words in the most exquisite and apt English imaginable. It was in this translation work that his powers of interpretation came frequently into play, and scholars in the original languages often found their understanding increased after studying Shoghi Effendi's English translations.

His genius was not confined to his English, however, for his attention to detail when giving the different teaching plans to National Assemblies; his concept and design of the gardens round the Shrine of the Báb on Mount Carmel and around Báhjí, 'Akká; his understanding of human nature as seen when counselling and inspiring people of all classes and religious backgrounds, and the simplicity of his personal life, were all part of the uniqueness of Shoghi Effendi, the first and only Guardian of the Bahá'í Faith.

He died of Asian flu while visiting London with his wife in November 1957 and is buried in the New Southgate Cemetery, London N11. Through his life and works however, the Guardianship of the Bahá'í Faith remains as one of the 'twin pillars' of the World Order of Bahá' u' lláh.

The Universal House of Justice

Although Bahá'u'lláh had clearly given the laws and ordinances to his followers and these have been carefully explained and interpreted by his successors there would be a continuing need for authoritative rulings on the application of these laws and teachings to an ever-evolving society and on matters not clearly specified in Bahá'í Scripture. Bahá'u'lláh made provision for this in his writings by instituting an elected body to be known as the Universal House of Justice.

A small section of the Bahá'í Gardens, Haifa

The grave of the Shoghi Effendi in the New Southgate Cemetery, London N11

68

It is incumbent upon the members of the House of Justice to take counsel together regarding those things which have not outwardly been revealed in the Book, and to enforce that which is agreeable to them. God will verily inspire them with whatsoever he willeth, and he verily is the Provider, the Omniscient.[65] (Bahá'u'lláh)

Unto the Most Holy Book everyone must turn, and all that is not expressly recorded therein must be referred to the Universal House of Justice. That which this body, whether unanimously or by a majority doth carry, that is verily the truth and the purpose of God himself.[66] ('Abdu'l-Bahá)

In clarifying still further the powers of this Supreme Body, 'Abdu'l-Bahá in his Will and Testament continued:

Inasmuch as the House of Justice hath power to enact laws that are not expressly recorded in the Book and bear upon daily transactions, so also it hath power to repeal the same... This it can do because these laws form no part of the Divine Explicit Text.[67]

'Abdu'l-Bahá's Will therefore provided for all contingencies—a Guardian of the Faith with powers of interpretation of Scripture and the elected Universal House of Justice to give authoritative decisions on the application of the laws and on all matters not recorded in Bahá'í Scripture. Writing on these twin institutions in 1934 the Guardian said:

The interpretation of the Guardian, functioning within his own sphere, is as authoritative and binding as the enactments of the International House of Justice, whose exclusive right and prerogative is to pronounce upon and to deliver the final judgment on such laws and ordinances as Bahá'u'lláh has not expressly revealed. Neither can, nor will ever, infringe upon the sacred and prescribed domain of the other. Neither will seek to curtail the specific and undoubted authority with which both have been divinely invested.[68]

It was not until the one hundredth anniversary of the Declaration of Bahá'u'lláh (21 April 1963) that the conditions were right for the election of this important body and on that date, in Haifa, at the World Centre of the Bahá'í Faith, representatives of the fifty six National Spiritual Assemblies then in existence, performed the task, as anticipated by Bahá'u'lláh himself and as spelled out in detail by 'Abdu'l-Bahá.

Under its guidance the Bahá'í World Community continued expanding at an increasing rate and the unity of the Faith and its singleness of purpose have remained unimpaired. Whereas man-made institutions tend to be more prone to divisions as their basic membership increases, the Bahá'í Administrative Order, due to its unique scriptural origin, becomes more stronger, more united, more efficient as its world-wide membership grows.

In 1972 the Universal House of Justice published its own Constitution which embodied all the specific scriptural provisions for its foundation, its powers and duties. In the by-laws of this Constitution details were given of the nature of an International Convention which would be held every five years to elect the members of the Universal House of Justice.

In April 1978, the fourth International Convention was held in Haifa, when delegates from 123 National Adminstrative bodies recorded their votes. Among those present were two illiterate National Spiritual Assembly members—one a carpenter from a primitive tribe in South America and the other a woman from one of the Pacific Islands. The presence of these two among the many hundreds gathered at that Convention and who represented an amazing variety of racial, religious and cultural backgrounds further demonstrated how, in this World Order of Bahá'u'lláh, all people may play their part, not merely at local and national levels but even in the International Convention which elects and consults with the supreme administrative body of the Bahá'í World Community.

Hands of the Cause of God
References were made in Bahá'í Scripture to the appointment of a very select group of Bahá'ís who would be chosen to give outstanding service to the Cause. In His Will and Testament, 'Abdu'l-Bahá explained how they would be appointed and the duties they would perform.

The Hands of the Cause of God must be nominated and appointed by the Guardian of the Cause of God. All must be under his shadow and obey his command.[69]

The obligations of the Hands of the Cause of God are to diffuse the Divine Fragrances, to edify the souls of men, to promote learning, to improve the character of all men and to be, at all times and under all conditions, sanctified and detached from earthly things. They must manifest the fear of God by their conduct, their manners, their deeds and their words. This body of the Hands of the Cause of God is under the direction of the Guardian of the Cause of God. He must continually urge them to strive and endeavour to the utmost of their ability to diffuse the sweet savours of God, and to guide all the peoples of the world, for it is the light of Divine Guidance that causeth all the universe to be illumined.[70]

Thirty two Hands of the Cause were appointed by Shoghi Effendi during the years 1951–57.

It was as 'Chief Stewards' that the Hands of the Cause of God took over the reigns of the affairs of the Cause after the sudden and unexpected passing of Shoghi Effendi in 1957, until the Universal House of Justice was elected in 1963.

International Convention, Haifa, Israel 1978

Auxiliary Board Members

In April 1954, the Guardian called upon those Hands of the Cause then appointed to select, in each continent and from among the resident Bahá'ís of that continent some believers, to be known as 'Auxiliary Board Members' who would 'act as deputies, assistants and advisers of the Hands'. These Auxiliary Board Members worked directly under the guidance of the Hands of the Cause and although subject to the overall requirements of the Bahá'í administration were not involved in it.

Continental Boards of Counsellors

According to the Will and Testament of 'Abdu'l-Bahá, the Guardian had to appoint his successor from among his descendants but Shoghi Effendi had no children nor was there anyone who could measure up to the high standards indicated in the Will. It was also clear that only the Guardian could appoint Hands of the Cause.

When the Universal House of Justice was elected in 1963, one of its first tasks was to examine Bahá'í Scripture and the writings of Shoghi Effendi to see if there was any provision at all for another Guardian. If there could be no Guardian who would arrange for the appointment of more Hands of the Cause? On 6 October 1963, the following announcement was made:

> After prayerful and careful study of the Holy Texts bearing upon the question of the appointment of the successor to Shoghi Effendi as Guardian of the Cause of God and after prolonged consultation which included consideration of the views of the Hands of the Cause of God residing in the Holy Land, the Universal House of Justice finds that there is no way to appoint or legislate to make it possible to appoint a second Guardian to succeed Shoghi Effendi.[71]

In November 1964 the Universal House of Justice further announced that after giving its full attention to the matter and studying the Sacred Texts and hearing the views of the Hands of the Cause themselves, it had arrived at the following decision:

There is no way to appoint, or to legislate to make it possible to appoint, Hands of the Cause of God.

Responsibility for decisions on matters of general policy affecting the institution of the Hands of the Cause, which was formerly exercised by the beloved Guardian, now devolves upon the Universal House of Justice as the supreme and central institution of the Faith to which all must turn.[72]

In 1968 the Universal House of Justice announced the formation of eleven 'Continental Boards of Counsellors', three boards each for Africa, the Americas and Asia and one each for Europe and Australasia and wrote: 'Their duties will include directing the Auxiliary Boards in their respective areas, consulting and collaborating with National Spiritual Assemblies, and keeping the Hands of the Cause and the Universal House of Justice informed concerning the conditions of the Cause in their areas.'[73]

This decision immediately freed the Hands from the administration of the Auxiliary Boards and the letter from the Universal House of Justice made the position quite clear:

The Hands of the Cause of God are one of the most precious assets the Bahá'í world possesses. Released from administration of the Auxiliary Boards, they will be able to concentrate their energies on the more primary responsibilities of general protection and propagation, 'preservation of the spiritual health of the Bahá'í communities' and 'the vitality of the faith' of the Bahá'ís throughout the world.[74] (24 June 1968)

International Teaching Centre
In June 1973 the Universal House of Justice announced the formation of yet another institution for this continually expanding community. Anticipated in Bahá'í Writings this new body would consist of all the Hands of the Cause around the world plus three Counsellors and would, among its other duties:

Co-ordinate, stimulate and direct the activities of the Continental Boards of Counsellors and act as liaison between them and the Universal House of Justice.
   Be fully informed of the situation of the Cause in all parts of the world and be able, from the background of this knowledge, to make reports and recommendations to the Universal House of Justice and give advice to the Continental Boards of Counsellors.
   Be alert to possibilites, both within and without the Bahá'í community, for the extension of the teaching work into receptive or needy areas, and to draw the attention of the

Universal House of Justice and the Continental Boards of Counsellors to such possibilities, making recommendations for action.[75]   Universal House of Justice

Local Spiritual Assemblies
In his writings, Baha' u' llah had referred on many occasions to the local Houses of Justice. In his Book of Laws he wrote: *'The Lord hath ordained that in every city a House of Justice be established wherein shall gather counsellors to the number of Baha (9). It behooveth them to be the trusted ones of the Merciful among men and to regard themselves as the guardians appointed of God for all that dwell on earth.'*[76]
'Abdu'l-Baha referred to these bodies as 'Spiritual Assemblies' and in one passage wrote:

> *. . . These Spiritual Assemblies are shining lamps and heavenly gardens, from which the fragrances of holiness are diffused over all religions, and the lights of knowledge are shed abroad over all created things. From them the spirit of life streameth in every direction. They, indeed, are the potent sources of the progress of man, at all times and under all conditions.*[77]

The formation of local Spiritual Assemblies is therefore a goal for every group of Baha'is the world over and in enlarging upon their function the Universal House of Justice wrote in April 1974:

The divinely ordained institution of the Local Spiritual Assembly operates at the first levels of human society and is the basic administrative unit of Baha' u' llah's World Order.

It is concerned with individuals and families whom it must constantly encourage to unite in a distinctive Baha'i society, vitalized and guarded by the laws, ordinances and principles of Baha' u' llah's Revelation. It protects the Cause of God; it acts as the loving shepherd of the Baha'i flock.

Strengthening and development of Local Spiritual Assemblies is a vital objective... and will demonstrate the solidarity and ever-growing distinctiveness of the Baha'i community, thereby attracting more and more thoughtful souls to the Faith and offering a refuge to the leaderless and hapless millions of the spiritually bankrupt, moribund present order...

The friends are called upon to give their whole-hearted

support and cooperation to the Local Spiritual Assembly, first by voting for the membership and then by energetically pursuing its plans and programmes, by turning to it in time of trouble or difficulty, by praying for its success and taking delight in its rise to influence and honour. This great prize, this gift of God within each community must be cherished, nurtured, loved, assisted, obeyed and prayed for.

Such a firmly-founded, busy and happy community life as is envisioned when Local Spiritual Assemblies are truly effective, will provide a firm home foundation from which the friends may derive courage and strength and loving support in bearing the Divine Message to their fellow-men and conforming their lives to its benevolent rule.[78] (Universal House of Justice, April 1974)

The local Spiritual Assemblies are, except in special cases, elected annually on the first day of the Riḍván Festival (i.e. from sunset 20 April to sunset 21 April). The members are elected by secret ballot, without any nominations or canvassing, from among all the adult believers in the town, village, district or other area for which the Assembly will be responsible. These areas vary from country to country but are always the smallest recognized civil administrative unit of that country. (In the United Kingdom the unit is the District or the London Borough.)

In March 1923 Shoghi Effendi spelled out some of the duties of these Spiritual Assemblies:

The matter of Teaching, its direction, its ways and means, its extension, its consolidation, essential as they are to the interests of the Cause, constitute by no means the only issue which should receive the full attention of these Assemblies . . .

They must endeavour to promote amity and concord amongst the friends, efface every lingering trace of distrust, coolness and estrangement from every heart, and secure in its stead an active and whole-hearted cooperation for the service of the Cause.

They must do their utmost to extend at all times the helping hand to the poor, the sick, the disabled, the orphan, the widow, irrespective of colour, caste and creed. They must promote by every means in their power the material as well as the spiritual enlightment of youth, the means for the education of children, institute whenever possible, Bahá'í educational institutions, organize and supervise their work and provide the best means for their progress and development . . .[79]

National Spiritual Assemblies
'Abdu'l-Bahá when describing in his Will and Testament how the Universal House of Justice should be elected, referred to 'secondary Houses of Justice' and in 1923 the Guardian called upon certain countries to form National Spiritual Assemblies. From his letter we read:

> Its immediate purpose is to stimulate, unify and coordinate by frequent personal consultations, the manifold activities of the friends as well as the local Assemblies; and by keeping in close and constant touch with the Holy Land, initiate measures, and direct in general the affairs of the Cause in that country.
>
> It serves also another purpose, no less essential that the first, as in the course of time it shall evolve into the National House of Justice . . . which according to the explicit text of the Testament will have, in conjunction with the other National Assemblies throughout the Bahá'í world, to elect directly the members of the International House of Justice, that Supreme Council that will guide, organize and unify the affairs of the Movement throughout the world . . .[80]

In the years that followed, more and more National Assemblies came into existence and gradually, through the guidance given to them by the Guardian, their functions became clear and they gained in strength and authority. As soon as possible after the formation of a National Spiritual Assembly it seeks to obtain a legal identity and it becomes 'incorporated in whatever way is possible best to embody the universal standards for such Bahá'í administrative bodies as are clearly described in Bahá'í Writings. Local Assemblies may similarly be incorporated as this is further evidence of their stability and permanence.

The National Administrative body in the British Isles has been in existence for over fifty-five years, being responsible until 1972 for the whole of the British Isles, then subsequently, with the formation of the National Spiritual Assembly of the Bahá'ís of the Republic of Ireland, being concerned only with the affairs of the United Kingdom. It was incorporated in 1939.

CONVENTION

National Assemblies the world over are elected by delegates who normally meet at a National Convention during the Riḍván Festival (i.e. between 21 April and 2 May). The Convention has three main functions; firstly to receive the reports of the outgoing National Assembly, secondly to elect the new National Assembly, and thirdly to consult with the incoming Assembly.

OFFICERS

All Assemblies, National and local, elect by majority vote from their nine members the offices of Chairman, Vice Chairman, Secretary and Treasurer, but no officer has any powers other than those given by the Assembly itself.

BAHÁ'Í ELECTIONS

The pattern of Bahá'í elections set by the Guardian in his early letters to the American Bahá'í Community is so completely different from anything we can find in the world of politics that it is worthy of close examination. The elections are yet another aspect of the distinctive nature of Bahá'í life. They bring about a balance between authority and freedom which can be found in none of the existing political systems of the world for with the supreme authority of the Word of God on the one hand and the absolute freedom of the individual to vote for whomever his conscience leads him to choose on the other, a system of ideal government at local, National and International levels is found in the Bahá'í World Community.

The voter, quietly and in a prayerful attitude, secretly records his vote, is free from any pressure and is confident of the rightness of the outcome when all the votes are counted. Whoever is elected by the method of plurality voting which is adopted throughout the Bahá'í world at all levels (except for the majority vote used for Officer elections), is immediately and wholeheartedly accepted by the electorate. The following paragraph written in 1925 primarily for delegates at a National Convention sets a standard for all Bahá'í elections at whatever level:

How great the privilege, how delicate the task of the assembled delegates whose function it is to elect such national representatives as would by their record of service ennoble and enrich the annals of the Cause! If we but turn our gaze to the high qualifications of the members of Bahá'í Assemblies, we are filled with feelings of unworthiness and dismay, and would feel truly disheartened but for the comforting thought that if we rise to play nobly our part every deficiency in our lives will be more than compensated by the all-conquering spirit of his grace and power. Hence it is incumbent upon the chosen delegates to consider without the least trace of passion and prejudice, and irrespective of any material consideration, the names of only those who can best combine the necessary qualities of unquestioned loyalty, of selfless devotion, of a well-trained mind, of recognized ability and mature experience.[81]

(Shoghi Effendi)

High administrative standard

Once elected, the members of every Bahá'í administrative body have before them a standard to achieve which seems almost impossible to attain but which is the goal of every Assembly whether it be among the sophisticated peoples of London, New York, Tokyo, Ṭihrán or Buenos Aires or among the Pygmies in the jungles of Central Africa, the Lapps in Finland or the Aborigines of Australia. The following quotations touch briefly on some of the elements of this high standard:

Let us . . . remember that at the very root of the Cause lies the principle of the undoubted right of the individual to self-expression, his freedom to declare his conscience and set forth his views . . .

Let us also bear in mind that the keynote of the Cause of God is not dictatorial authority but humble fellowship, not arbitrary power, but the spirit of frank and loving consultation. Nothing short of the spirit of a true Bahá'í can hope to reconcile the principles of mercy and justice, of freedom and submission, of the sanctity of the right of the individual and of self-surrender, of vigilance, discretion and prudence on the one hand, and fellowship, candour, and courage on the other.

The duties of those whom the friends have freely and conscientiously elected as their representatives are no less vital and binding than the obligations of those who have chosen them. Their function is not to dictate, but to consult, and consult not only among themselves, but as much as possible with the friends whom they represent. They must regard themselves in no other light but that of chosen instruments for a more efficient and dignified presentation of the Cause of God. They should never be led to suppose that they are the central ornaments of the body of the Cause, intrinsically superior to others in capacity or merit, and sole promoters of its teachings and principles. They should approach their task with extreme humility, and endeavour, by their open-mindedness, their high sense of justice and duty, their candour, their modesty, their entire devotion to the welfare and interest of the friends, the Cause, and humanity, to win, not only the confidence and the genuine support and respect of those whom they serve, but also their esteem and real affection. They must, at all times avoid the spirit of exclusiveness, the atmosphere of secrecy, free themselves from a domineering attitude, and banish all forms of prejudice and passion from their deliberations.

They should, within the limits of wise discretion, take the friends into their confidence, acquaint them with their plans, share with them their problems and anxieties, and seek their advice and counsel. And, when they are called upon to arrive at a certain decision, they should, after dispassionate, anxious and cordial consultation, turn to God in prayer, and with earnestness and conviction and courage record their vote and abide by the voice of the majority, which we are told by our Master to be the voice of truth, never to be challenged, and always to be wholeheartedly enforced. To this voice the friends must heartily respond, and regard it as the only means that can ensure the protection and advancement of the Cause . . .

Let it be made clear to every inquiring reader that among the most outstanding and sacred duties incumbent upon those who have been called upon to initiate, direct and coordinate the affairs of the Cause, are those that require them to win by every means in their power the confidence and affection of those whom it is their privilege to serve. Theirs is the duty to investigate and acquaint themselves with the considered views, the prevailing sentiments, the personal conviction of those whose welfare it is their solemn obligation to promote . . . [82]

(Shoghi Effendi)

Nineteen Day Feast
It will be seen later that in the Bahá'í Calendar there are nineteen months and on the first day of the month there is held a most

unique type of meeting. Essentially it is an administrative occasion for it is the time when the local Spiritual Assembly consults with its community, acquaints the community of its plans and seeks consultation on the affairs of the community. This meeting is called a 'Nineteen Day Feast'. Although the feast consists of three separate parts they are arranged so that the whole occasion is one of great spiritual upliftment and helps to deepen the unity of the friends. Only registered Bahá'ís may be present at a Nineteen Day Feast and Bahá'ís who are not in their home community are encouraged to attend the Nineteen Day Feast of the place they are visiting. The first part of the Feast is essentially devotional and appropriate selections from Bahá'í Scripture are read, sung or chanted, this period is followed immediately by the consultation period under the direction of representatives of the local Spiritual Assembly, reports are made on the various activities of the local Assembly and any of its committees and by the Treasurer on the state of the local fund. When the consultation period is concluded the friends have refreshments which may vary from a simple glass of water to a substantial meal.

The Nineteen Day Feast is therefore yet another quite distinctive feature of the Bahá'í community and part of the life of every Bahá'í.

It is of interest to note that a child or infant may be registered as a Bahá'í by its parents and will be instructed in the laws, teachings and history of its Faith. He will be encouraged to study religion widely and know the basic elements and history of all the world's religions. At the age of fifteen the Bahá'í child must then assume his responsibilities as a Bahá'í (though as we have seen he may not vote in Bahá'í elections until he reaches the age of 21). A child, even of Bahá'í parents, who has not by the age of fifteen expressed the wish to become a member of the Bahá'í community and declared his or her belief as a Bahá'í, may not attend a Nineteen Day Feast.

Where a Bahá'í community has joyous, vigorous and fruitful Nineteen Day Feasts it is certain that that community will be active, growing and completely united.

Assistants to Auxiliary Board Members
It should be noted that Hands of the Cause and Boards of Counsellors work directly with National Spiritual Assemblies. Auxiliary Board members work closely with local Assemblies and individual believers. The Hands and the Counsellors, being

Bahá'í Temple, Sydney, Australia

appointed respectively by the Guardian and by the Universal House of Justice are not part of the 'elected side' of the Administrative Order and do not stand for election to the National Assemblies. Board members are, however encouraged to appoint 'Assistants' to carry out specific tasks for them and these Assistants may remain on any administrative body to which they are elected or any committee to which they have been appointed, either by a local, or by the National Assembly.

On 1 October 1969 the Universal House of Justice further clarified the respective roles of elected and appointed members as follows:

It is the responsibility of Spiritual Assemblies, assisted by their committees, to organize and direct the teaching work, and in doing so they must, naturally, also do all they can to stimulate and inspire the friends. It is, however, inevitable that the Assemblies and committees, being burdened with the administration of the teaching work as well as with all other aspects of Bahá'í community life, will be unable to spend as much time as they would wish on stimulating the believers.

Authority and direction flow from the Assemblies, whereas the power to accomplish the tasks resides primarily in the entire body of the believers. It is the principal task of the Auxiliary Boards to assist in arousing and releasing this power. This is a vital activity, and if they are to be able to perform it adequately they must avoid becoming involved in the work of administration . . . [83]

It is to help the the Auxiliary Board members 'to assist in arousing and releasing . . . the power to accomplish the tasks' and to encourage the believers to turn spontaneously to their Auxiliary Board members for inspiration and to the Assemblies for guidance and direction, that the work of the Assistants is directed.

Committees, local and National

Members of local and National Assemblies are elected for the qualities of loyalty, devotion, ability and experience, but they are rarely specialists in every field of community activity. Committees of experts are therefore appointed.

All committees are responsible only to the Assembly which appointed them. They meet, elect their officers, consult on their activities, carry out their specific terms of reference and report as required to the administrative body which appointed them.

Leadership therefore in the Bahá'í Community is not found in individuals but in the elected administrative bodies and these bodies seek to use the expertise, the zeal and the enthusiasm of the members of the community so that all believers may fully participate in whatever field their interests lie. This personal involvement and commitment is another exciting and distinctive aspect of Bahá'í life.

The Twin Pillars

Chapter 2, 'How the Bahá'ís live', shows that there are two 'sides' to the world-wide Administrative Order of Bahá'u'lláh. On the one hand is the 'appointed' side with the Guardian of the Bahá'í Faith appointed in the Will and Testament of 'Abdu'l-Bahá; the appointment by the Guardian of the Hands of the Cause; the appointment by the Universal House of Justice of the Counsellors, who in turn appoint Auxiliary Board members and who in their turn appoint their Assistants. On the purely administrative side the rank and file of the believers elect their local Spiritual Assemblies and their delegates, their delegates elect the National Assemblies and the members of the National Assemblies elect the members of the Universal House of Justice.

The Guardian of the Bahá'í Faith in his letter of 8 February 1934, subsequently published under the title *The Dispensation of Bahá'u'lláh*, spoke of the two institutions of the Guardianship and the Universal House of Justice as the 'Twin Pillars that support this mighty administrative structure'. In the next paragraph of that same letter he wrote:

. . . These twin institutions of the Administrative Order of Bahá'u'lláh should be regarded as divine in origin, essential in their functions and complementary in their aim and purpose. Their common, their fundamental object is to ensure the continuity of that Divinely-appointed authority which flows from the Source of our Faith, to safeguard the unity of its followers and to maintain the integrity and flexibility of its teachings. Acting in conjunction with each other these two inseparable institutions administer its affairs, coordinate its activities, promote its interests, execute its laws and defend its subsidiary institutions. Severally, each operates within a clearly defined sphere of jurisdiction; each is equipped with its own attendant institutions—instruments designed for the effective discharge of its particular responsibilities and duties.[84]

In explaining still further the Universal House of Justice wrote in 1965:

> Unity of doctrine is maintained by the existence of the authentic texts of Scripture and the voluminous interpretations of 'Abdu'l-Bahá and Shoghi Effendi, together with the absolute prohibition against anyone propounding 'authoritative' or 'inspired' interpretations or usurping the function of Guardian. Unity of administration is assured by the authority of the Universal House of Justice. 'Such', in the words of Shoghi Effendi, 'is the immutability of his revealed Word. Such is the elasticity which characterizes the functions of his appointed ministers. The first preserves the identity of his Faith, and guards the integrity of his law. The second enables it, even as a living organism, to expand and adapt itself to the needs and requirements of an ever-changing society.'[85]

Finally as we look at this unique pattern for a 'New World Order' we see how it fulfils 'the practical realization of those ideals which the prophets of God have visualized, and which from time immemorial have inflamed the imagination of seers and poets in every age'. These words were taken from one of the earliest 'World Order' letters addressed by Shoghi Effendi to the Bahá'ís of the West; it was actually written in 1930. It deals specifically with the differences between the Bahá'í Faith and the ecclesiastical organizations of other religions and this chapter could well close with a few more sentences from this highly significant letter.

> Bahá'u'lláh . . . has not only imbued mankind with a new and regenerating Spirit . . . he, as well as 'Abdu'l-Bahá after him, has . . . clearly and specifically laid down a set of Laws, established definite institutions, and provided for the essentials of a Divine Economy. These are destined to be a pattern for future society . . . and the one agency for the unification of the world, and the proclamation of the reign of righteousness and justice upon the earth . . .[86]

The Bahá'í Fund

With the rapid spread of the Bahá'í Faith around the world, the building of its beautiful Houses of Worship in all the continents, and the purchase of many thousands of local and national Bahá'í

Bahá'í House of Worship, Wilmette, USA

Centres or Headquarters, with many hundreds of national and local endowments, Bahá'í Schools, training institutes and other institutions, the question is often asked 'Where does all the money come from?'

Only Bahá'ís may contribute to the Bahá'í Fund. No teaching may be done, no property purchased, no endowment established and no Bahá'í activity may be carried out with monies except those which have come from a recognized Bahá'í source. To contribute to the Bahá'í Fund is an obligation upon every Bahá'í. The amount he or she gives, when it is given, in what form the donation takes, whether it be given for the general use of the administrative body to which it is donated or whether it is earmarked for a special purpose, are all left to the conscience of the individual believer. The giving is done quietly, even secretly, from the individual to the local, national or international Treasurer.

The Bahá'í House of Worship, Frankfurt, Germany—by night

Should a non-Bahá'í try to insist on giving a contribution it would be made clear that such monies could not be used for the work of the Bahá'í Faith, but would be donated to some charity. Shoghi Effendi wrote:

I feel urged to remind you of the necessity of ever bearing in mind the cardinal principle that all contributions to the Fund are to be purely and strictly voluntary in character. It should be made clear and evident to everyone that any form of compulsion, however slight and indirect, strikes at the very root of the principle underlying the formation of the Fund ever since its inception . . . [87]

The supply of funds . . . consititutes . . . the life-blood of those nascent institutions which you are labouring to erect. Its importance cannot, surely, be over-estimated. Untold blessings shall no doubt crown every effort directed to that end...[88]

We must be like the fountain or spring that is continually emptying itself of all that it has and is continually being refilled from an invisible source. To be continually giving out for the good of our fellows undeterred by the fear of poverty and reliant on the unfailing bounty of the Source of all wealth and all good—this is the secret of right living.[89]

Bahá'í Houses of Worship

In the days to come there will be Bahá'í Houses of Worship in every town and village but at the moment they are only being built on the basis of one per continent or island group, though many temple sites have been purchased for future development. With a membership which is relatively small it is considered more important to give most of the Bahá'í contributions to help spread the Faith and to assist the poor and uneducated believers in the developing countries. This leaves the building of beautiful Houses of Worship for the future when many more millions have embraced the Faith. The Houses of Worship already built, or in the process of being built, demonstrate the new concepts of worship and are only being built on a continental basis and then gradually developed as examples of what these institutions will be like in the future.

There will be a central House of Worship which will be nine-sided, have its doors open to all peoples of all races and will be domed. Within its walls only the human voice will be raised either singing, chanting or reading and no musical instruments will be used. Only selections from the Holy Scriptures of different religions will be used and no preaching or administrative activity will take place in the House of Worship.

Bahá'í House of Worship, Wilmette, USA

As the institution develops there will be built around the central House of Worship accessory buildings such as a school for Science, a Hospice, a Hospital and a Home for Orphans. In other words, the House of Worship, according to Bahá'í understanding, caters not only for the spiritual needs of the community it serves but also its social, educational and humanitarian needs. Its proper name in Arabic means 'Dawning-place of the praise of God'.

Presently there are completed Houses of Worship in Wilmette, USA; Kampala, Uganda; Frankfurt, Germany; Sydney, Australia; and Panama City, while plans have been made for Houses of Worship in India and Western Samoa. The Wilmette Temple has one dependency—a Home for the Aged, and in Wilmette, Kampala and Frankfurt the National Headquarters are in the vicinity of the Central House of Worship.

The Bahá'í House of Worship, Frankfurt, Germany

The Bahá'í Calendar

There is a surprising number of Calendars in use around the world and it is essential, if real world unity is to be achieved, that there should be one Calendar that is recognized and acceptable the world over. It is an essential part of the distinctive Bahá'í life that all the Bahá'ís the world over observe, in their religious activities, a Calendar which was inaugurated by the Báb. This Calendar brings some entirely new ideas in the measurement of time and the fixing of dates. The solar year was adopted but it begins, like the ancient Persian new year and the modern Iranian Naw-Rúz, with the March Equinox (21 March). It is therefore astronomically fixed and the Bahá'í era commences with the year of the Declaration of the Báb (1844).

In the Bahá'í year there are nineteen months of nineteen days each, making a total of 361 days, so between the eighteenth and nineteenth month there are four or five 'intercalary days'; the nineteenth month is a month of fasting in preparation for the celebration of the New Year's Day (Naw-Rúz). The Báb named the months after the attributes of God and the Bahá'í day starts and ends at sunset.

The names of the nineteen months are as follows:

Month	Arabic Name	Translation	First Days
1st	Bahá	Splendour	21 March
2nd	Jalál	Glory	9 April
3rd	Jamál	Beauty	28 April
4th	'Azamat	Grandeur	May 17
5th	Núr	Light	5 June
6th	Rahmat	Mercy	24 June
7th	Kalimát	Words	13 July
8th	Kamál	Perfection	1 August
9th	Asmá'	Names	20 August
10th	'Izzat	Might	8 September
11th	Mashíyyat	Will	27 September
12th	'Ilm	Knowledge	16 October
13th	Qudrat	Power	4 November
14th	Qawl	Speech	23 November
15th	Masá'il	Questions	12 December
16th	Sharaf	Honour	31 December
17th	Sultán	Sovereignty	19 January

| 18th | Mulk | Dominion | 7 February |
| 19th | 'Alá | Loftiness | 2 March |

During the year there are special feasts and anniversaries as well as the days of fasting, and these are listed as follows:

Feast of Riḍván (Declaration of Bahá'u'lláh) 21 April–2 May 1863
Feast of Naw-Rúz (Bahá'í New Year), 21 March
Declaration of the Báb, 23 May 1844
Day of the Covenant, 26 November
Birth of Bahá'u'lláh, 12 November 1817
Birth of the Báb, 20 October 1819
Birth of 'Abdu'l-Bahá, 23 May 1844
Ascension of Bahá'u'lláh, 29 May 1892
Martyrdom of the Báb, 9 July 1850
Ascension of 'Abdu'l-Bahá, 28 November 1921
Period of the Fast, 19 days beginning with the first day of the month of 'Alá, 2 March

During the Bahá'í Year there are nine Holy Days on which all work is suspended. Three of these are in the period which commemorates the Declaration of Bahá'u'lláh and there is one for the Declaration of the Báb. Others celebrate the Birthday of Bahá'u'lláh and the Birthday of the Báb while two commemorate the deaths of Bahá'u'lláh and the Báb. The ninth one is the New Year's Day.

Relations with the non-Bahá'í world
Much emphasis has been paid in this part of the book to the distinctive character of the Bahá'í life and the way the Bahá'í community functions and observes its special Calendar. It must not be thought, however, that the Bahá'ís seek to work in seclusion or form 'communes' or are in any way isolated from their fellow human beings. On the contrary, they seek at all times to be fully involved in whatever activity seems to serve the best interests of their fellow-men and of mankind as a whole. They are constantly having to assess the allocation of their time, for on the whole they are very involved and active individuals. When they are young they have the burning desire to do well in their schooling so that they can make the maximum contribution to society. At the same time, however, they are eager to have their Bahá'í youth activities, attend week-end schools, summer schools and go out 'travel teaching' for their Faith,

An unusual Bahá'í Winter School programme

both at home and overseas. Many young Bahá'ís use the opportunity of the long school holidays to visit Bahá'í communities in areas which do not frequently receive outside visitors, and many of the Bahá'í youth from the United Kingdom have travelled in Europe, Africa and South America, while some have even been travel teaching in India and Malaysia. In assessing the allocation of their time, Bahá'ís must also be aware of the need to participate as fully as possible with movements that are also actively furthering the well-being of mankind.

At a local level the Bahá'ís are frequently active with the branches of the United Nations Association or of UNICEF, and others try to establish branches of the World Congress of Faiths and participate eagerly in all kinds of inter-faith activities.

At a national level Bahá'ís are also involved in working with the United Nations Association, UNICEF, the World Congress of Faiths, the Standing Conference of Inter-Faith Dialogue in Education, the Religious Education Council, the Association of World Federalists and other similar organizations that are absolutely universal in their approach. If any organization with which the Bahá'ís are associating becomes involved in any partisan or political activity or begins to take sides in any way, by showing some preference to one ideology or the other, to east or west, to black or to white, then the Bahá'ís will withdraw their support, they will not sponsor, nor give their backing to any activity which seeks to promote the interests of just one group.

It is in the arena of international affairs that some striking developments have taken place in recent years. In the spring of 1947 the National Spiritual Assembly of the Bahá'ís of the United States and Canada was accredited to the United Nations Office of Public Information (OPI) as a national non-governmental organization qualified to be represented through an observer. A year later, however, eight such National Assemblies were collectively recognized as an International Non-Governmental Organization under the title 'Bahá'í International Community'.

On 27 May, 1970, the Bahá'í International Community was granted consultative status by the Economic and Social Council (ECOSOC) and on 8 March 1976, was officially accredited with the United Nations Children's Fund (UNICEF).

The Bahá'í International Community works closely with ECOSOC, its functional commissions, committees and other associated bodies. It has participated in United Nations Years, in major UN conferences concerned with the social and economic problems of the planet, such as those on Human Environment, Population, Food, Status of Women, Crime Prevention, Human Settlements, and Water, and in many regional conferences and seminars. For all these activities it produces statements on world issues of concern to the United Nations which are circulated as official UN documents and it has published several brochures. These not only offer the Bahá'í approach to life and society, but suggest the application of certain Bahá'í principles to specific world problems.

It would be fitting to close this relatively brief textbook on the Bahá'í Faith with a quotation from one of the documents produced by the Bahá'í International Community in June 1977. It is from a section dealing with the contribution of the world-wide Bahá'í community to the ideals of the United Nations Charter:

> In the basic areas of motivation and attitude, the Bahá'í International Community is making a valuable contribution towards improving the quality of life of all people—essential for the achievement of universal human rights and world peace. For instance:
> 1.   Bahá'í communities have gained considerable experience in eliminating all forms of prejudice in pursuance of the Bahá'í

principle of the organic oneness of humanity and the systematic abolition of prejudice and discrimination. Bahá'í communities educate their members concerning the positive values and contributions of all religions in order to eradicate religious prejudice. They also assert the full dignity of the individual regardless of ethnic background; and the conviction that there is but one human race has guided the actions of their members concerning rights and responsibilities.

2.　Bahá'í communities are helping to overcome the obstacles of tradition and superstition which prevent many people from benefiting from the improvements of science and technology; because the Bahá'í teachings, from which Bahá'í communities draw their beliefs and strength, see no conflict between religion and social and economic development. In addition, Bahá'ís are taught that religion must work hand in hand with science.

3.　Furthermore, the Bahá'í Faith stresses the importance of the mind of man, since it is this consciousness that differentiates him from the animal. The human mind must be properly educated, spiritually and materially.

4.　Consequently, Bahá'í communities have fostered the principle of universal compulsory education by establishing primary and secondary schools open to children of all backgrounds and beliefs in places where educational facilities are not available. In addition, these communities have established adult education programmes in basic literacy and community development.

5.　Arts and sciences are praised, and Bahá'ís are enjoined to dedicate themselves to those areas of human knowledge that do not begin and end in words, but are of benefit to mankind . . .

Finally, since Bahá'í communities are concerned with developing in each person his highest potentialities—besides love, compassion, and justice, the moral qualities of honesty, trustworthiness, truthfulness—as well as ensuring that such qualities will be reflected in social action and interaction—the results of this education are bound to have an impact beyond the Bahá'í environment. Such values, firmly linked as they are in Bahá'í communities with a consciousness of the interdependence of all peoples and the goal of one world united in peace, provide the fundamental motivation for action in solving the problems of our world. (Bahá'í International Community, 1977)

Bibliography

'Abdu'l-Bahá' (H. M. Balyuzi)   George Ronald 1971
Advent of Divine Justice (Shoghi Effendi)   Bahá'í Publishing Trust Wilmette, Illinois, USA 1939
*Compilation No. 7 'Bahá'í Education'   Bahá'í Publishing Trust United Kingdom 1976
Bahá'í Journal of the United Kingdom
Bahá'u'lláh and the New Era (Esslemont)   BPT 1974
*Bahá'í Prayers for Special Occasions   BPT 1975
*The Bahá'í Revelation 1955 (out of print)
*Bahá'í World Faith 1956 (out of print)
*Compilation No. 2 'Continental Boards of Counsellors'   BPT 1969
*Covenant of Bahá'u'lláh   BPT 1963
The Dawn Breakers   BPT 1975
Epistle to the Son of the Wolf (Bahá'u'lláh)   BPT, USA 1941
*Faith for Every Man   BPT 1972
God Passes By (Shoghi Effendi)   BPT, USA 1945
*Guidance for Today and Tomorrow (Shoghi Effendi)   BPT 1953
Gleanings from the Writings of Bahá'u'lláh   BPT 1978
Hidden Words (Arabic) (Bahá'u'lláh)   BPT 1975
*Compilation No. 3 'Lifeblood of the Cause'   BPT 1970
*Compilation No. 1 'Local Spiritual Assemblies'   BPT 1970
*Living the Life   BPT 1974
*Compilation No. 5 'National Spiritual Assemblies'   BPT 1972
Paris Talks ('Abdu'l-Bahá)   BPT 1972
Selections from the Writings of 'Abdu'l-Bahá   Bahá'í World Centre, Haifa 1978
Tablets of 'Abdu'l-Bahá Vol II (out of print) 1915
Wellspring of Guidance (Universal House of Justice)   BPT, USA 1969
World Order of Bahá'u'lláh (Shoghi Effendi)   BPT, USA 1938

*Are compilations from Bahá'í writings.
BPT = Bahá'í Publishing Trust, 2 South Street, Oakham, Rutland.

References

Chapter 1

1 The Dawn Breakers p.19, 2 *ibid* p.40, 3 *ibid* p.40, 4 *ibid* p.42, 5 *ibid* p.41, 6 *ibid* p.44, 7 *ibid* p.44, 8 *ibid* p.45, 9 *ibid* p.49, 10 *ibid* p.65, 11 *ibid* p.373, 12 *ibid* p.375, 13 *ibid* p.376, 14 Epistle to the Son of the Wolf p.141, 15 The Dawn Breakers p.445, 16 *ibid* p.461/2, 17 God Passes By p.101, 18 *ibid* p.102, 19 *ibid* p.101, 20 Gleanings from the Writings of Bahá'u'lláh p. 254, 21 Bahá'u'lláh and the New Era p.37, 22 Gleanings from the Writings of Bahá'u'lláh p.223, 23 Selections from the Writings of Abdu'l-Bahá p. 27.

Chapter 2

24 Gleanings from the Writings of Bahá'u'lláh p.216, 25 Paris Talks pp.129/130, 26 God Passes By p.217, 27 Paris Talks p.129, 28 God Passes By p.217, 29 Gleanings from the Writing of Bahá'u'lláh p.216, 30 *ibid* p.139, 31 *ibid* p.213, 32 Abdu'l-Bahá p.141, 33 Gleanings from the Writings of Bahá'u'lláh p.49, 34 *ibid* pp.51/52, 35 Advent of Divine Justice p.31, 36 *ibid* p.31, 37 Selections from the Writings of Abdu'l-Bahá p.291, 38 Paris Talks p.143, 39 *ibid* p.131, 40 *ibid* p.53, 41 *ibid* p.129, 42 Bahá'í World Faith p.341, 43 Gleanings from the Writings of Bahá'u'lláh p.165, 44 *ibid* p.47, 45 *ibid* p.62, 46 Hidden Words (Arabic) p.4, 47 Gleanings from the Writing of Bahá'u'lláh p.77, 48 Hidden Words (Arabic) p.32, 49 Gleanings from the Writings of Bahá'u'lláh p.155/156, 50 *ibid* p.148/149, 51 Tablets of 'Abu'l-Bahá p.98, 52 Gleanings from the Writings of Bahá'u'lláh p.249, 53 Bahá'í Prayers for Special Occasions p.44, 54 *ibid* p.44, 55 Bahá'í World Faith p.364, 56 Living the Life p.42, 57 Tablets of 'Abdu'l-Bahá Vol. II p.474, 58 Faith for Every Man p.63, 59 The Bahá'í Revelation pp.291/2, 60 Paris Talks p.162, 61 Bahá'u'lláh and the New Era p.141, 62 Bahá'í Education p.83, 63 Guidance for Today and Tomorrow p.168, 64 *ibid* pp.173/4.

Chapter 3

65 Guidance for Today and Tomorrow p.86, 66 *ibid* pp.86/7, 67 *ibid* p.87, 68 *ibid* pp.87/8, 69 Covenant of Bahá'u'lláh p.101, 70 *ibid* pp.101/2, 71 Wellspring of Guidance p.11, 72 *ibid* p.41, 73 *ibid* p.141, 74 *ibid* pp.142/3, 75 Bahá'í Journal No. 218 p.2, 76 Local Spiritual Assemblies, p.3, 77 *ibid* p.3, 78 Bahá'í Journal No. 222 p.2, 79 Local Spiritual Assemblies p.9, 80 National Spiritual Assemblies p.1, 81 *ibid* p.3, 82 *ibid* pp.18/9, 83 Covenant of Bahá'u'lláh pp.17/9, 84 Guidance for Today and Tomorrow pp.84/5, 85 Wellspring of Guidance p.53, 86 World Order of Bahá'u'lláh pp.19/20, 87 Lifeblood of the Cause p.4, 88 *ibid* p.9, 89 *ibid* p.12.

Index

Administration, Admin,
Order, 63–6,70,72–6,78,80,82,83
Alcohol, 53,61
Auxiliary Board Members, 72,73,80,82,83

Bahá'í International Community
5,92,93
Behaviour, 51

Calendar, Bahá'í, 79,89,90
Chastity, 54
Children, 50,54,56–60,75,80,93
Civilization, 5,38,41,44,55,59,61
Community Life, 75,80,82,83,88,93
Continental Board/Counsellors,
72,73,74,80,83

Death, 47–9
Deeds, 51,71
Divorce, 55
Drugs, 53,61

Education, 57–9,75,93
Elections, Bahá'í, 75,77,78,82,83
Equality of Sexes, 57–9
Evil, 50,51
Evolution, 39,50,54

Family, 53–6, 74
Fasting, 51,52,64,89,90
Free Will, 47
Funds, 80,84–7
Future Society,
60,61,64,65,74,75,84,87,89,92,93

God, 5,10,11,14,15,19–22,23,27,30,
36–8,40–3,45–54,57,59,62,63,65,
69–75,77,78,79,84,89
Nature of, 45,46,47,50
Good, 50,51,62
Government, 53,60,64,77
Guardian of the Faith (Shoghi Effendi)
32,55,60,61,65–72,75–9,82–4,86

Hands of the Cause of God, 70–3,80
Happiness, 34,54
Harmony Religion/Science, 43,46
Heaven/Hell 48
Houses of Worship, 48,49,52,63,81,84–8

International Auxiliary Language, 60
International Teaching Centre, 73

Justice, 47,78,79,93

Kingdom of God, 63
Knowledge, 59,74,93

Laws, 51,53,54,61,67,69,70,80,83,84
Leadership, 83
Life After Death, 47,48,53
Literacy, 59,93
Love, 38,40,46,47,51,52,54,57,58,93

Man, 47–50,93
Marriage, 53,54,56,57
Mercy, 47,78

Nineteen Day Feast, 79,80

Oneness of
Humanity, 39,40,42,53,56,62,93
Oneness of Religion, 40–3

Patriotism, 53
Poverty, 51,60,62,86
Prayer, 51,52,64,72,77,79
Prejudice, 42,43,60,61,78,79,92,93
Prohibitions, 61,84
'Promised One', 7,10,11,13,14,26

Religion/Science, 43,44,60,93
Riḍván Festival, 26,75,77,90

Science, 43,44,59–61,88,93
Secret Ballot, 75,77
Sex, 54,55
Soul, 47–9
Spiritual Assemblies,
66,74–8,80,82,92

Teaching the Faith,
53,63,65,73,75,79,80,85,93
Truth, 43–5,47,51,69

United Nations, 5,92,93
Unity, 30,39–44,45,59,61,83,84,89
Universal House of Justice,
65,67,69–76,82,83,84

Wealth, 60,86
Women, 56–9,65,92
World Civilization, 5,40,59
World Commonwealth/Parliament/
Government, 59,60
World Community, 65,70,77,92
World Order/Peace,
5,30,42,53,57,67,74,92,93
Worship, 52,53,59,64